OUTSIDE Influences

OUTSIDE
Influences

*Catalytic Concepts
for Understanding
How Life Really Works*

Adam Ginsberg

NEW YORK

LONDON • NASHVILLE • MELBOURNE • VANCOUVER

OUTSIDE Influences
Catalytic Concepts for Understanding How Life Really Works

© 2020 Adam Ginsberg

Published in New York, New York, by Morgan James Publishing. Morgan James is a trademark of Morgan James, LLC. www.MorganJamesPublishing.com

ISBN 978-1-64279-477-9 paperback
ISBN 978-1-64279-478-6 eBook
Library of Congress Control Number: 2019933436

Cover Design by:
Rachel Lopez
www.r2cdesign.com

Interior Design by:
Bonnie Bushman
The Whole Caboodle Graphic Design

In an effort to support local communities, raise awareness and funds, Morgan James Publishing donates a percentage of all book sales for the life of each book to Habitat for Humanity Peninsula and Greater Williamsburg.

Get involved today! Visit
www.MorganJamesBuilds.com

To my phenomenal wife Lori,

Without you, this would not have been possible.

Without you, I would not be the person I am today.

Without you, I couldn't possibly understand what true love really is.

Without you, I would be lost.

You have been, are now, and forever will be, my inspiration, motivation, best friend and guiding outside influence!

Table of Contents

Introduction

I have always believed in a contemplative, reflective approach to life. Many people go through life taking each day as it comes, without much thought about the dynamic forces that shape our lives. I must admit to seeing a certain wisdom in that simple approach but it is just not a path that's open to me. The process of thoughtful consideration occasionally yields conceptual gems, but is always valuable in and of itself. We expand ourselves through mental and philosophical exercise as we consider the world in all of its wonder and grandeur. *Outside Influences* is full of what I call "catalytic concepts." These are ideas that will stimulate your thinking and stretch your mind.

I'm not a person who readily accepts the status quo. I have always challenged the generally accepted approach and forced justification and rationalization from the common wisdom. I don't do things because that's how they've always been done, and I refuse to think about life in a certain way because that's how people have always thought about it. My inability to conform has gotten me in hot water through the years, but has also yielded many interesting experiences and perspectives.

Outside Influences is not intended to turn your world upside down or provide some sort of mind-altering experience (although be sure to message me on social media if it does!). It doesn't contain "The Irrefutable Laws of Success" or "The Master Keys to Self-Motivation" or the "6 Habits That Will Change Your Life."

Rather, my goal is to have you consider the question of an underlying force in life and develop and appreciation for how outside factors influence impact what you achieve and how you live. Mostly I want it to be an enjoyable, stimulating and enlightening experience that ends up in dinner table, business meeting, and water cooler conversation.

The experiences that have brought me to writing this book have been diverse, challenging and exciting. I have started several companies. Four have become successful. Two extraordinarily so. I've work with thousands of different personalities over the course of my career in different businesses, in different industries. Through three decades (it is amazing how quickly time passes) I have been very fortunate to have worked with some really terrific people. In everything I've done, I've always paid careful attention to the human dynamics in the equation.

As in life, my approach to writing *Outside Influences* has been holistic. A successful life is multifaceted, including family, career, wellness, recreation, community, as well as our spiritual and philosophical sides. Because a well-defined philosophy toward life and business should acknowledge our spiritual side, I also offer some (potentially controversial) ideas in that arena. I am deeply respectful of the religious beliefs of others. How we all choose to relate to our spiritual side (if at all) is an important and personal matter.

I believe this applies to both individuals and organizations. In one of the companies I worked closely with, the clearly defined company philosophy centered on people, products and programs. The philosophical approach to the business—which became the foundation for future businesses that I started—had a philosophical approach holding the contributions of people in the highest esteem. Massive amounts of resources and energy were put into recognizing people for their contributions and efforts.

Although I live in the United States, I've had the distinct privilege to travel extensively around the world and meet (and work) with people from all walks of life and all backgrounds. The forces behind *Outside Influences* are not exclusive to the United States, far from it. They are systemic to the world at large and apply equally across the globe.

This is not a textbook or scientific treatise although some of the topics might seem complex and overwhelming. I took a responsible approach because the subject matter deserves it. I gave proper attribution and I tried to lay down a logical, sometimes passionate argument. But I confess, I've been cursed with a somewhat sarcastic sense of humor that is impossible to turn off. I believe we can have a lot of fun while accomplishing serious tasks, so I'm giving you fair warning, you'll find humor (always to the point and never in bad taste) sprinkled throughout the book making for an enjoyable read.

Outside Influences is not a traditional motivational book, although many people have reported that the ideas are motivating to them. It's not meant to be instructional but rather to be stimulating. I specifically and intentionally set out to write a book that presented a new idea about life and how the world works. I wanted to offer a different and refreshing perspective on an element of life that has gotten little, if any, attention. And how this idea can ultimately impact your success.

Most of what has been written about life and success deals with the internal factors that lead to a specific set of results and outcomes and it's entirely appropriate that we examine and consider those, but that's not my purpose here. What I've addressed are some of the dynamic forces that swirl around us, outside of ourselves, that also bear on the direction and outcome of our lives. The goals here are growth, expansion, elucidation and understanding. *Outside Influences* was written to stimulate your thinking, not change your behavior or get you to take action on a "to do" or "how to" list.

Finally, I'd like to take a moment to define "success" as it's used in the context of the book. To me, success is happiness, fulfillment, personal growth, meaningful accomplishment and freedom. *Happiness* comes from a rich and full personal life with ample time for the ones we love. It also comes from enjoying whatever work we have chosen, the people we work with, and our work environment. *Fulfillment* comes from personal growth, the individual spiritual path we take toward maturity, enlightenment and peace. *Growth* results from expansion of our knowledge, skills and most importantly, understanding of the world around us. *Meaningful accomplishment* yields a sense of satisfaction from making a contribution to our family, our community, our company, and society at large. It's about giving back, making a difference, and leaving the world a better place in even a small personal way. And freedom comes from financial results. Money doesn't buy happiness, but does have an impact on your ability to travel, do as you want, with the people you want to do it with, as often as possible.

In a real way, success is a deeply personal destination. *Outside Influences* has been written with the assumption that we all move through life with a healthy tension between where we are now, and where we want to be. It's the journey that makes up the stuff of life and this book focuses on factors affecting the outcome of the adventure. To a degree, our ethos of success handicapped us because some of the previously unacknowledged facts about the way life unfolds have been minimized or obstructed from view. I want to shine a spotlight on those factors.

Understanding the terrain can help you get to where you want to go. Will following the principles in *Outside Influences* absolutely guarantee success? Well, I'm aware that other authors make such claims about their books, but out of respect for your intellect, I won't give you any false promises. It would be antithetical to do so since part of the message of the book is that nothing can guarantee success. What I believe *Outside Influences* will do is to expand your understanding and open up new lines of thought and consideration for you. Over time, that should provide significant help in your travels through life.

So, let's get started.

CHAPTER 1

The Traditional Success Paradigm

"Truth is the breath of life to human society. It is the food of the immortal spirit."

–Oliver Wendell Holmes

The model to achieving success is well documented and widely accepted. It's hard to imagine there could be some new secret that could be uncovered within the generally accepted paradigm.

A few years ago, a published article about golf great Tiger Woods promised an in-depth examination of his winning ways to "shed light on the science of winning." The prescription? Work very hard, have confidence, surround yourself with coaches and mentors, and have a strong desire for success. Not exactly earth-shattering information. Maybe the secret to success is that it's not that complicated—but the truth is that the success paradigm has a lot of holes in it. There are many really good motivated, determined, educated, hard-working, passionate, smart people with a positive attitude who never reach big time success. There is a flaw with this conventional wisdom.

Know the Rules of the Game

It's hard to win at a game if you don't know all the rules. In the realm of what we do, we want to understand the rules and object of the game, how the game works and how to win. Imagine the frustration of playing a game where the rules are constantly changing, or where new rules come into effect that you weren't aware of. In game play, we've all admonished competitors at one point or another, by saying "You can't make up the rules as you go along!"

Yet life does this to us all the time. Most people go through life with a very limited understanding of all the factors that impact them. Interestingly, we readily accept the personal onus of our part of the equation, yet we ignore the effects of many other influences, beyond our control. We think by ignoring them they will go away, but they don't. Throughout the book I will refer to these occurrences as *Outside Influences*.

The better your "knowledge of the game" the greater your chance of success. It's just that simple. A competent accomplished person considers all influential factors, even the small ones, while navigating through life. An inclusive perspective is wise and valuable. One who discounts, ignores or denies key factors is born of ignorance and limits possibilities.

The more you know, understand and acknowledge about how life works, the greater your potential.

We Should Seek Truth

The mysteries of life fascinate and frustrate us as we search for the path to success, fulfillment and happiness. Curiosity may have killed the cat, but it serves us well. It stimulates us to want to learn, grow and understand. Most of us begin our search to make sense of the world at an early age, and the search continues as long as we have our faculties. The beauty and wonder of it all seem limitless. For many, it's the process of searching, in and of itself that gives life meaning. The discovery of new perspectives further entices us to explore.

The gates at Harvard University are emblazoned with the Latin word "Veritas," which means truth. A commitment to search for the truth is a noble yet extremely difficult task. There is so much misinformation out there. In the broadest context we have all identified mysteries that are beyond our comprehension; even the learned struggle. Compared to all that is understandable, even the brightest of the bright among us is trying to light a vast dark desert in the pitch black of night, with a small flickering candle. What we can know and understand is dwarfed by the mysteries of the cosmos and perhaps always will be.

But there are important concepts we can grasp. There are specific strategies we can implement. There are identifiable systems we can put in place. Along with truth we celebrate many other great ideas such as justice, wisdom, duty, courage, integrity, beauty, confidence, love, honor, eternity and God. Our history as a people are replete with the evidence of a person's growing knowledge, wisdom and philosophy. The constellation of great ideas is awe-inspiring. Our capacity for deep thought and contemplation provides strength and satisfaction.

As we make our way through life we discover and will be confronted by many perspectives, strategies, belief systems, facts, opinions and ideas. We synthesize these to form our own point of view.

We draw from many perspectives, but there are of course dominant sources that contribute significantly. Our parents, our siblings, our spouse, the news media, social media and the society we live in all make major contributions, creating a patchwork of ideas that becomes our unique perspective. Human nature being what it is, we tend to be open to and embrace evidence that reinforces what we believe. If facts or ideas contradict our belief systems, we usually ignore or discount them. It takes an enlightened and confident person to consider a contrary point of view, even when it is supported by dramatic evidence.

In writing this book, I was searching for the truth about the dynamic forces that shape our lives. I reasoned that a better understanding of the mechanics of life, of human nature, and the real processes for success, is a worthwhile benefit. I wanted to know for the sake of knowing. And now I want as many people as possible to know as well. What I've discovered will help us navigate the path we travel. The way I see it, the more you know and understand about how the world really works, the better suited you are to find happiness and reach high levels of success.

If you've ever stepped back, looked at the world in all of its whirling, swirling, evolving, illogical glory and scratched your head in amazement you're going to love this book. For all of life's senseless, irrationality, and fairness, if we look deeply enough we can see an underlying dynamic system that reveals a certain (chaotic) order and identifiable dynamic forces. The world follows rules and you can learn from them.

The search for truth often turns inward. Personal growth can yield many benefits. Truth is complete. The more we know about our environment and ourselves the greater the wisdom, and the better able we are to manifest our wonderful potential.

The Quest for Success

It's inherent in human nature to strive for success, and a few things are more fun than being in hot pursuit of your goals. Part of what makes life worth living is the quest many of us carry on each day to accomplish something extraordinary. The quest for success is not about a bigger house, beautiful clothes, a nicer car or a private jet (they're nice, but there's more to it). The quest for success is also about achievement. It's about overcoming obstacles. Living life to the fullest is more about giving, accomplishing, and creating than it is about accumulating. My goal in writing *Outside Influences* is to help you achieve the quest for success in your life by better understanding how one aspect of the system of life works.

This book is not about "dumb luck", which as you know is a very real thing. The quest for success is interwoven in all aspects of life—but the key to long term sustained growth is understanding the dynamics of success. What is the system? How do we reach the summit? What is the path?

This "search for the truth" is so much a part of human nature that in some cultures people spend the better part of their lives searching for "enlightenment" or understanding. Far be it for me to suggest that I have the way to enlightenment or mindfulness; I'll leave that to others. I want to broaden your understanding of how one facet of life (and success as it's optimum expression) works.

Isn't it wonderful that there is such a thing as success? I mean it's really possible for the average person to live a life that is the stuff of dreams. Perhaps you know someone who is, or has. Perhaps you are doing so right now. Most likely you are not—yet. But… It's also likely that your desire to do so runs deep and certainly you want to go to the next level, whatever that means for you.

I believe in people. I do not believe that people who don't achieve their goals are not motivated. Most of us carry deep inside a desire for accomplishment and achievement. We instinctively seek to improve ourselves and circumstances for our families. It's been my experience that this quest is widespread.

A highly motivated human being is a powerful force. When we strive for accomplishment we tap into inner strength and talent not otherwise available to us. Desire for success ignites genius and fortifies us for the effort. By definition, a quest is the pursuit of a worthwhile goal with some significant meaning for you. People on a quest do not go to "work" each day. They are usually engaged in an activity they thoroughly enjoy. When you love what you do, it's a passion, not a chore. It will require choices, to be sure, but they aren't really sacrifices because you're doing what you prefer to do.

Achievement requires focus and concentration. It's a good way to gauge your level of intent to see what you are ready, willing and able to give up. Distractions go by the wayside when you're on a quest, in pursuit of your dreams. If you find yourself torn, wanting to do other things, feeling disappointment for your lack of diversion, you are not on a true quest. When you are, you don't watch the clock and you don't work an eight-hour day. A quest occupies all of you, most notably, your imagination and creativity. It could be said that being on a quest will bring out the entrepreneurial spirit in you.

The world presents so much evidence to each of us every day of the potential for human achievement. It is key to remember that people who accomplish extraordinary things are just people, as you or I. You don't have to be a superhuman to be successful—superhumans exist only in comic books and in the movies, but ordinary people can be inspired to do extraordinary things when they set out to create something special or overcome a significant challenge. As you work to achieve your quest, it works on you as a source of inspiration and as an invitation to greatness.

Sometimes you must set out on a quest to find a quest. I've always considered it an amazing good fortune to find something you truly love, are good at, and can profit from. Any one of those things is hard to find, and to find all three in one place is rare, indeed. An engagement of your talents and skills that challenges you, brings out your best efforts and pays big dividends is unique and valuable. If you have been so blessed, release your brakes and pursue your quest with every fiber of your being. If you are still searching, perhaps the ideas in this book will trigger something valuable for you. The search for your passion (which could be starting your own business, having a family, or playing a sport is a worthwhile effort. You'll know your passion when you see it, and you'll find joy and satisfaction in the activity itself. Finding the quest that's right for you is a big part of the battle. If your quest is does not include financial gain, you'll still need focus on the financial aspects of your life to best support your question.

Though the power of the quest for success is universally accepted, the path to achievement is shrouded in mystery. Thousands of books have been written, videos recorded, and seminars given on the keys to success based on the premise the that we alone can control direction and outcome of your life. Perhaps you've heard of "Personal Power"? There are countless stories of people who have overcome significant challenges, people who went against all odds and were victorious. These individuals inspire us and encourage us to follow in their footsteps. Their examples reinforce the idea that our life is in our hands and what we accomplish is completely up to us. Yet, it's an incomplete formula.

For thousands of years, the vast majority of the population pretty much generally accepted that life happens to you. The notion that people could control the course and quality of their lives just didn't match the realities of everyday life. They contracted complex belief systems to answer life's unanswered questions. Perhaps life moved at the whims of the gods, or destiny, or some combination of supernatural forces. In 60 AD Marcus Annaeus Lucanus said, "I have a wife, I have sons; all of them hostages given to fate." Only a very few people at the extreme top of the ladder had any real influence over the direction of their lives, and even they regularly made sacrifices to the gods and consulted oracles. People were seen, for the most part, as floating helplessly down the raging river of life, sometimes being dashed against the rocks, occasionally making it through to placid peaceful waters. It was widely accepted that influences beyond our control ruled the day, determining our destiny.

When bad things happened, people saw it as their fate and could only bemoan the outcome. The vast majority of people struggled through life, looking outside of themselves for comfort, guidance and direction. People thought there was very little they could do to affect the outcome of their lives, and a great deal of evidence supported that idea. Self-determination was the province of only the wealthiest humans—the rulers.

In the nineteenth century, philosophies about life and success began to move away from the idea that we are at the mercy of the fates. Coincident with the Industrial Revolution, more people started to exert influence over their lives, and the idea of personal responsibility began to emerge. The pendulum of thought began to swing from a point of view that had little control over our lives to one in which we might have control. William James (1842—1910), the noted American philosopher and psychologist and the originator of the doctrine of pragmatism, observed and promoted this phenomenon when he stated, "It has been the greatest discovery of this generation that man can control his own destiny." For a century and a half this idea has flourished and gained momentum. Writing his noteworthy book, *As a Man Thinketh*, published around 1901, author James Allen postulated, "All that a man achieves and all that he fails to achieve is the direct result of his own thoughts."

The litany of success is everywhere. "If it is to be, it's up to me." "Whether you think you can, or you think you can't, you're right." It's pervasive in modern day society. Movies like "The Secret", "Think and Grow Rich" and "Rudy", Books like *"Predictable Success", "Self-Made Success", "The Success Code"* and *"Man Up"* to stories like the *Little Engine that Could* ("I think I can, I think I can") to Horatio Alger to the US Hockey Team in the 1980 Olympics, validate this point. We all love a story about someone who overcomes adversity and achieves success. This is what made the *Rocky* movie franchise so successful. How can we forget, when at the end of movie, Rocky Balboa (played by Sylvester Stallone) voices the words, "Yo Adrian, we did it." We are entertained and inspired by these stories, the message resonates and is fully integrated into our thinking about the world and about success. We love this idea of success.

As it is prone to do—as seen at any Tony Robbins live seminars—the pendulum of thought has swung a little too far. I like Tony Robbins. I believe he is the best in the world at what he does. However, I don't believe that success can simply be achieved by jumping for hours and screaming the word "YES" as you ramp up to a peak state. In a broad sense, when thought starts to move to an extreme point of view, it tends to overshoot the target, swinging to the opposite extreme. We've gone from thinking our lives are largely controlled by influences beyond our control to thinking we are full control of the direction and outcome of our lives. Eventually, over time, if a pendulum is not powered to continue swinging, it will come to rest in the middle. Conceptual balance seems the proper approach here.

The Contradictions

The idea that we can make whatever we want from our lives is exciting, but the problem is that the reality seldom fits the hype. Big time success with all the abundance is not easy, yet I believe that most people can achieve their goals. However, the foolproof formula has some holes in it and it leaves thinking people wondering about the path to success and happiness. It's not right to say that we are at the mercy of fate—that life just happens to us as we flail away meaninglessly. But the notion that we are in total control of our lives (and our destiny) seems equally incorrect when you consider all the evidence.

Emerson said, "Most people lead lives of quiet desperation". I'm not sure I fully agree, but certainly there is some truth to this observation. At retirement-age many people look back on at least a portion of their lives with a sense of disappointment. They feel that they could have, perhaps should have, accomplished more. Coupled with that disappointment can be feelings of inadequacy, because where the pendulum sits now, you are in control of your life and responsible for its outcome. So, if it didn't turn out the way you would have liked, you have nobody to blame but yourself.

What do we tend to think about people who have not achieved success? They must not have worked hard enough. They are probably lazy. Maybe they are not too bright. Perhaps they don't have any real talent. It could be they are not meticulous enough, couldn't manage their money or their time.

For whatever reason, they were not worthy of success or they would have achieved it, right?

It's my carefully considered opinion that most of what we think and have been taught about life, career and success is partially wrong. The core notion of how to achieve success that emerged early in the twentieth century, that we control our own destiny and make our own success, is only partially correct. Napoleon Hill became famous by propagating the idea that "Whatever the mind of a person can conceive and believe, it can achieve." It's a wonderful thought and it's motivated many people to high levels of success. The only problem is that it's not entirely accurate.

Now part of the beauty of this philosophy is that it has a built-in qualifier. To any person who conceives an idea, believes in it, and goes after it only to get their teeth knocked in, Mr. Hill would reply, "Well, see, you didn't believe enough. You let doubt creep in and that was your undoing." Or, there's the classic, "You just weren't motivated enough." This dramatic oversimplification has caused a great deal of frustration for a lot of people. Motivation is linked to desire. If a person wants something he or she is by definition motivated to go after it. It takes a lot more than just desire and motivation to reach success. Achievement in even the simplest of human endeavors is very complex, with many factors affecting the outcome of our efforts.

It would be great if life or success in life could be reduced to one simple statement, one simple straightforward formula, but it can't. And it can't be summarized in 7 or 8 simple steps. The purpose of this book is to help you understand that the contradictions between what we are told will happen when we "follow the program" and the realities of how life actually work are acute and stark. The ideas in *Outside Influences* are intended to reconcile what we want to believe is necessary in our pursuit of success with evidence of what is really going. This yields a workable, understandable approach that still acknowledges the joy of achievement and our contribution to it, but factors in some new ideas about the uninvited encroachment of the world on our plans. The objective is to leave with a complete picture, a plan based on all facets of a system designed to achieve the ultimate in success. It's a big goal, but I'm confident we will achieve it. And if you believe it… you can… _____. I'm sure you can fill in the blank.

The contradictions can be vexing and frustrating. We're told to get a good education and then we graduate into a stagnant job market. We're told that hard work will pay off, so we work our tail off only to meet with indifference from our superiors. We're told to take risks and the economy goes into free fall. Now it is possible to overcome these and many other challenges and come out a winner, but our ability to do so starts with understanding the rules of the game. There's a reason for the contradictions and that's what this book is about—shedding light on a previously ignored part of the success equation.

Outside Influences

Many outside factors, beyond our control, influence the direction and outcome of our lives. The series of events, activities and experiences we call life emerge from the interplay of our thinking, initiative, decisions and actions with innumerable outside influences that affect our environment and are often beyond our comprehension or awareness.

The evidence for these outside influences is everywhere, yet, for the most part, we have totally ignored them in our lexicon of success. We can continue to gloss over their existence and basically pretend they are not really there. Or, we can face them, examine them, study them and develop a well-considered approach to life that encompasses an understanding of the impact of issues beyond our control. I'm suggesting a slightly different approach to how success works. Success does not come to people just because they are hard-working, talented and smart. The vast majority of people are good, bright, capable and diligent. But most of those people do not reach big time success. They don't get to enjoy life's unlimited bounty. Something else is at work there.

Most of us can recite the commonly accepted "principles of success:" Get a good education, choose a growth field, find something you are passionate about, work hard, sacrifice, stay motivated… pretty much everybody knows what they are supposed to do. And in my experience, most people, in fact do those things on a regular basis. The world is full of very smart, hard-working, wonderfully talented smart broke people who never really get ahead. They participate in the rat race, pay their dues, do their duty and fade away.

The frustration that builds for a person who has not achieved his or her dreams can be massive. It's why coaches and mentors are so important. It's one thing for someone who doesn't play by the rules not to achieve success. But the majority of honest, good people who want the best for themselves and their family, are frustrated with their lack of success. Perhaps you are one of those people? Most assuredly, you know many of them.

The Success Paradigm

Our traditional model for achieving success in well documented. I'll refer to you books by Tony Robbins, Grant Cardone, Dr. Eric Thomas, Brendon Burchard. I want to state clearly and categorically that of all the factors that affect success, those within our control, are the most influential. These inside influences can be learned. They can be studied. They can be implemented. And with a mentor, they can be obtained. Without a mentor you significantly reduce your chances for success.

The old philosophy has served us pretty well and the "inside influences" such as our motivation, hard work, determination, enthusiasm and fortitude are important. I don't intend to dispel the old paradigm, but to amend it. Complete it. Success in life can never be guaranteed, regardless of the amount of hard work or goal setting or time management you implement. You can acquire 70 habits if you like. You can try to learn *The Secret*. You can put yourself into a positive state. You can pound your chest and chant ancient proverbs. And, unfortunately for people, it's not just about getting a good education or working for a great company. To a large degree, success is situational and life is not fair in its dispersal of affluence.

If you accept that life is not fair, and there are huge piles of evidence to support this, then you will begin to let in some light. Why isn't it fair? Why doesn't hard work always lead to success? Is there some fiendish plot to torture or frustrate us? Absolutely not. "Life" didn't come up with the idea that there's a direct relationship between our efforts and our rewards, we did. The desire for success is so acute that we want to believe despite so much evidence to the contrary. The way the system works is evident to anyone who is willing to challenge the status quo and simply ask a few questions. One key question is: why do we believe in a system that is failing so many people? Part of the answer is that the notion that we control our destiny in very reassuring, even if it's a mirage.

Success in life can never be guaranteed. But, neither can life itself. Yet there are things you can do to achieve a long, healthy life just as there are specific strategies you can implement to become successful.

The Need for Control

Most of us know at least one control freak, but we seldom consider our own desire for control. To acknowledge outside influences is not to give up what control we actually do have.

To pretend that there are no outside factors that affect us is to diminish our control, but the net effect is to reduce our control because operating under a false assumption undermines our self-determination.

The desire for control that we all have is actually a response to, and acknowledgement of, our awareness of outside influences. We can see that things outside of our awareness have an effect on our lives. But, since we cannot know what that effect may be, we've chosen to minimize or eliminate any consideration of it. We're afraid of the unknown, but the response I'm suggesting is to try to understand the nature of the many outside influences that come in to play, rather than ignore them.

Fear is a powerful and debilitating emotion. Our various responses to it range from total panic, letting the object of our fear force irrational actions and decisions, to complete denial, trying to neutralize the fear by pretending the object of our fear doesn't exist at all. The nature of owning a small business, for example, is that it has a certain (yet very manageable) set of risks but denial of the existence of them can increase our exposure. And with all of that, fear can also be an incredible motivator.

Now, there is something to be said for the hard-driving attitude that proclaims, "I don't care what the obstacles are, I'll overcome them." "Whatever it takes!" is the so-called high achiever's anthem. And you know what? Sometimes it works! And when it does, we remember it, and employ that attitude time and time again. The problem is, sometimes it doesn't work. Occasionally problems are so complicated, it's not a question of making something happen, it's a question of trying to figure out what exactly is happening and sometimes we don't ever establish that.

The paradox in all of this is that deep down we know we are not in full control. How could we be? What we have not done is analyze the situation well enough to understand and accept these influences are part of your journey in life. But we've built an intricate system of beliefs and denials to bolster the idea that we alone forge the direction of our success. We reason what we don't know won't hurt us, but unfortunately the reverse if often true.

 Catalytic Concepts

- Our ethos of success is well documented and widely understood.
- The success paradigm has significant flaws based on empirical data.
- People once believed that our fate was decided for us.
- The vast majority of people are good people who desire relevance and success in their lives, yet seldom find it.
- We are not subject to fate or destiny, nor do we wield total control over our lives. There's an elegant balance between both inside and outside influences.
- We are at our best when we are on a quest for something extraordinary.
- Most people know the "right" steps to achieve their goals and they regularly take them despite disappointments and frustrations. The paradox is real and the contradictions stark.
- The commonly accepted keys to success are potent but incomplete in that they do not acknowledge the influence of factors outside of our control

CHAPTER 2

Belief Systems

*"We believe what we want to believe and what makes us happy, but facts to
not cease to exist because they are ignored."*
–Aldous Huxley

T his chapter focuses on what we believe about the way the world works and
how people achieve success. First, we will explore the human need to believe
and the many aberrations of belief that exist. Many belief systems address
the super-natural because it is clouded in mystery, yet is seen by many as an
underlying force in life. Understanding why we want to believe and how we
develop belief systems in general will shed light on the beliefs we hold about the
path to success.

We Want to Believe
A belief is something we take on faith that is inherently unknowable (though
there could be a great deal of evidence to support it). As we build our unique

philosophy on life, belief is the mortar between the stones of knowledge, experience and information. Those stones are the strength of your philosophy; if you have too much "mortar" the philosophy will not serve you well. The more our lives are based on beliefs versus reality, the more exposure we have to unseen problems.

The human ability to believe fervently is a marvelous trait. It's a wonderful thing to behold when you engage someone in a dialog about their beliefs, as they will defend them mightily. We readily accept the total validity of what we believe; yet we can see with crystal clarity the inane and ridiculous beliefs of others (despite the fact that they are often remarkably similar to our own).

Belief is an important and positive aspect of human nature. Our beliefs give us hope (which of course does not spring eternal unless you water it). Beliefs are necessary because so much about success defies logic and factual analysis. Beliefs fortify us to take risks.

Our belief systems contribute to the illusion of control, or at least cause and effect. The notion that our lives happen without our total control scares the daylight out of us. So, we have built innumerable tools and belief systems in an attempt to understand why things occur. We want to explain where we have been, why things happened in the past, where we are going and what will occur in the future.

We've all heard the phrase, "Millions of people can't be wrong". People use this logic to support their beliefs. Sure, one person can make a mistake about a belief, maybe a handful could, or a couple of hundred. But it is impossible for millions of people to believe fervently in something that is not true or completely inaccurate? You bet it is. In fact, any student of history will tell you it happens all the time.

The fact of the matter is, our track record of believing isn't very good at all. The vast majority of beliefs held by the vast majority of people over the vast majority of history have turned out to be incorrect. Consider the most recent US election cycle. The vast majority of the people (at least according to CNN) said it would be impossible for Donald Trump to be nominated President of the United States. Once nominated, the vast majority of the people (at least according to CNN) said it would be impossible for Donald Trump to be elected President of the United States. As I'm sure you know, Donald Trump IS the president of the United States.

The Illogic of Logical Beliefs

Sometimes people try to use logic to fortify beliefs when it's faith that provides their foundation. But don't fall prey to the common practice of rationalizing your belief system with "objective analysis." Even if most of your belief system is drawn from analysis and fact, if you acknowledge that somewhere along the way you must make a leap of faith, then it's belief not knowledge. Now, as I've said, belief is fine, just don't let it masquerade as information when it's really inspiration. Belief, by definition defies logic, and mixing the two can produce a volatile, occasionally explosive, combination.

.You could argue that the propensity to believe has gone a little haywire in our species. Beliefs can run rampant and are often on a collision course with one another. Remember, in many cases, beliefs are sacred. Religious fanaticism is belief that's out of control and like a wild vine, will seek to choke out all other belief systems around it. Beliefs revolving around the supernatural particularly can become very dangerous because they block all other ideas from view.

Be sure to keep the distinction between articles of faith (belief) and articles of fact (knowledge) clear in your mind. Learning to identify belief when you bump into it will give you insight into human nature and human thought (or, the lack thereof). Dealing with someone's belief system dictates a different behavior. Trying to use logic to explain or deny beliefs is like trying to tighten a blot with a screwdriver. It's almost always futile to reason with someone about something they believe in. First of all, for belief systems to take hold and flourish it must be very well constructed. It's unlikely that there is any argument that has not been made a thousand times before, and a well-structured belief system probably has a very plausible (and well-rehearsed) response. People hold on tight to what they believe.

Belief systems are all around us, and for the most part, the "believers" are very comfortable in their beliefs. Sometimes they do not even recognize them as beliefs. Certain beliefs can be so well ingrained in society they are taken as fact.

The Royal Treatment

A monarchy is a form of government but it is also another example of a deeply ingrained, well-supported belief system. For Americans, the concept of royalty does not compute. We do not believe that some people are somehow ordained to be our leaders and us their humble servants. But it is interesting to look at this phenomenon and the traditions and manipulations that have kept it in place.

Most of us have some idea of the pomp and circumstance that surround people classified as royalty in present day as well as those of historical monarchies. Not long-ago monarchy was the predominant form of government. It's important to note that the vast majority of the people who lived in a monarchy gave it their total support. They believed in it. The "subjects" of the king were, for the most part, loyal and the majority would readily sacrifice their relatively insignificant lives to save the life of their king.

In modern military (and the modern corporation, for that matter) there's the saying "Rank has its privileges," but even a general must come under the rule of the king. The privileges of royalty are far-reaching, indeed. The monarch is a dictator with the power to levy taxes, make laws and declare war. Through the centuries, millions of Europeans died at the whim of kings who often sent troops into battle over deeply personal issues. Helen of Troy may have had the "face that launched a thousand ships," but only one guy got to kiss her goodnight each evening and thousands went to war just so he could.

Common people bow to the King and Queen. They are all-powerful and must be treated at all times with utmost request. You never turn your back on the king; you back out of the room facing front. And this treatment is not only afforded the king but also the entire royal family. If you ever get a chance to observe people interacting with royalty, it's amazing to watch. The protocol is precise as otherwise mature adults readily act like silly children waiting in line to see Santa. The remarkable thing about all of this is that kings and queens are people too, no different from you and me.

We can learn a lot about human nature by studying the concept of the monarchy. For the most part, it's been bred into people to want to be led. The majority of any king's subject willingly support him. Now, obviously, depending on the temperament of the king, it could be tantamount to suicide not to support him, but most people are very much onboard. Even in modern-day Britain where the royal family is largely ceremonial, the people still support them in luxury. The worldwide outpouring of sympathy over the death of Queen Elizabeth shows that we all get into the act a little. *Business Insider* magazine went as far as saying, "the death of Queen Elizabeth will be one of the most disruptive events in Britain in the past 70 years." She was 101 when she died.

But when you look at the history of monarchy, there wasn't always a royal family. There is no such thing as a royal bloodline that goes back to the beginning of the human race. Royalty is a man-made concept (and a great gig if you can get it) and belief is its underpinning.

It's easy to imagine how it arose. Sine we know there weren't always such things and kings and queens, we can conclude that somebody invented the concept. Early humans were tribal. The alpha male (the dominant one) would emerge to take a leadership position. As is still the case among humans today, the leader would retain his power only as long as he could defend it, and younger males would challenge it, as he grew older and weaker. When he could no longer defend his leadership position, it was taken away from him. From there it's not a big stretch to imagine that the alpha male would groom his offspring to take his place. This might well protect him from getting hit over the head with a club and reduce the trauma to the tribe as power was transferred to the next generation. New leaders would have the benefit of their ancestor's exploits to help build the mystique. Carry that process out for a few centuries and the hereditary line would pick up all of the trappings and grandeur of royalty along the way. The pomp and circumstance add to the illusion, and kings began to accumulate wealth that made their power even more real.

Remember, for the most part, going along with the charade is voluntary for the masses. From time to time the people rise up and say, "OK, enough is enough" and they oust a king or despot usually only to install another. Occasionally, a truly noble leader is willing to step aside to allow a democracy to emerge. But for the most part people, comfortable in their beliefs, go with the flow and don't rock the boat. That's why monarchies have existed for thousands of years.

What does any of this have to do with us here, today? It's obvious to present-day Americans, born and raised in a democracy, that no human being is inherently more valuable, more worthy of life's abundance, than any other human being. But, as a card-carrying member of the human race, you should recognize this propensity is in our nature, and your own. It's amazing what people are able to conjure, construct, believe and take as dogma. Once internalized, beliefs become part of our framework for understanding the world around us and all of its mystery.

The Religious Perspective

Religion tackles tough questions: How did we get here? Where did we come from? What is the purpose of life? What happens after we die? It offers us guidance, community and comfort. We don't stop to think of it this way, but religion is a belief system. It's a helpful way to relate to the supernatural and incomprehensible. Religion strengthens and supports us. There are hundreds of different religions today, and there have been thousands through the ages.

Most people realize that there are many different ways to relate to God. However, most religious people believe there is only one true religion—one correct way to worship. Now, I'm not going to attempt to determine which, if any, is the true religion, but there is an inescapable conclusion I wish to highlight. They can't all be right, at least in their assertion that they alone worship the "one true God." Yet among the believers are people who hold the doctrine of the religion singularly and who reject any contrary approach. They are certain, beyond any shadow of a doubt, and they all point fingers at the others and criticize them for believing in false gods or doctrines. Somehow, things aren't adding up! How can so many people have conflicting views yet be so convicted that everyone else is wrong.

I'm focusing on the human desire and capacity to believe. All you have to do is look at the world's religions to see that it is very possible for multitudes of human beings to believe fervently in things that are not true. If you lump all of its many denominations and branches together (despite their significant differences) Christianity is the largest religion in the world. As of mid 2018, of the world's total population of 7.44 billion, approximately one third (2.3 billion) are Christians. Most people figure the largest would be one of the Eastern religions, but since China is a communist country, the majority of its inhabitants no longer practice a religion (at least not openly). So, with one out of three humans on the planet practicing some form of Christianity, it's the most widespread and generally accepted faith.

Now, if Christianity is the one true religion (as almost all Christians believe) that means at least two thirds of the people on earth must be wrong in their religious beliefs. If it happens that one of the smaller religions is the one true religion, then the percentage is much higher. Simple math tells us, when it comes to religion, most people get it wrong. But that does not dissuade religious people one iota from their beliefs because they are sure they believe in the right religion—all of them.

And if others don't see the correctness of the one true religion, occasionally they will have to show the "infidels" the path to God. As many people have been slaughtered on earth in the name of "religion" as for any other reason (with the possible exception of greed, but it could be argued that's redundant.) Amazingly, people will resort to violence to propagate or defends religions that purport to stand for peace, love and understanding.

The Role of Religions

Nothing in this book is meant to directly contradict anyone's religious beliefs. I try to be respectful of any belief. A lot of people believe that God guides the daily events in our lives and in the source of success. In a sense, that is in accord with the idea of *Outside Influences*, since we are not God.

I feel compelled to address the role of religion because the thinking in *Outside Influences* speaks to the underlying dynamic forces in life—"In An Ever Changing World." Within the right framework, nothing here disputes the existence of God. What you perceive as God and what I perceive as God may be something quite different, but I surely acknowledge a higher power.

To help you understand where I'm coming from, let me give you a quick review of my perspectives on the subject. I believe in an omnipotent force that created the universe and the laws of nature, which keep order in this complex system. To my way of thinking, all you have to do is take in the awesome natural beauty of our little corner of the universe to sense that something initiated and guides it. The earth is a truly wondrous place and I constantly marvel at its diversity and beauty. I don't know how someone could consider the multitude of exquisite life forms, the power and might of the ocean, the beauty of a clear, crisp, bright blue afternoon sky, or the starlit nighttime heavens, and come to the conclusion that this all "just happened." I know I'm in pretty good company on this point because Albert Einstein is quoted as saying, "You will hardly find one of the profounder sort of scientific minds without a religious feeling of his own." (Reminder: Einstein wasn't an English major.)

On top of that, you've got to consider that there are hundreds of billions of stars like our sun in our galaxy and billions of galaxies like the Milky Way in the Universe. Most people conclude that some force (in my opinion beyond our comprehension) created, initiated, and guides all of it. (Maybe at the big bang—God sneezed!)

To me it seems that what He has done is create a beautiful system, which He allows to operate by the laws of the cosmos He created, and which we speak eloquently of His nature and grandeur every day. Life, the world and the universe continue to expand and manifest His glory based on the initial instant He set it all in motion. As I see it, since it was done right the first time, it doesn't require God's day-to-day micro-management. I do not believe in a paternalistic deity that is intimately involved in the day-to-day details of the lives of all 7.4K billion people on the planet. Not that it's beyond His power to do so. In fact, I believe the reverse is true. His power is so vast that it, and in fact His very nature, is way beyond our ability to understand. I don't know what He is, but I believe He is there. I believe He is everywhere at all times, even if that seems impossible.

Ancient Beliefs

The study of the history of the world's religions offers many insights into the human psyche and our need to believe in something. What I find fascinating is how we can clearly see the flaws and foolishness of other religions while we accept the complete and utter correctness of our own. Over time, we've created a whole class of bogus religions what we've now, in retrospect, relegated to meaninglessness. We look at the religions of our ancient ancestors with tongue in cheek as the futile attempts of a backward people to understand the mysteries of the universe. Even our term for them connotes their invalidity—pagan religions.

We call their ceremonies "rituals." We stipulate that their gods, since they don't count and aren't real, should be spelled with a lower case "g."

But these pagan religions and their extensive pantheons, customs and rituals represent exquisite examples of how otherwise really intelligent advanced civilizations can go off the deep end of the subject of what they believe guides the world. Let's look briefly at these four: the Egyptians, the Greeks, the Romans and the Incas of Central America.

The Egyptians built the pyramids about 4,500 years ago. That's 2,500 years before the time of Christ. They had an amazingly advanced civilization. Consider these facts about the great pyramid of Cheops, just one of many spectacular buildings they constructed. It has over 2,300,000 stones in it. The average weight of the stones is 2.5 tons. The large blocks used in the ceiling of the King's chamber weigh as much as 9 tons each and the total weight of all the stones is 6,500,000 tons. It covers 568,000 square feet, 13 acres or seven city blocks square.

It is said that to build the great pyramid today, with all of the modern-day technology available to us, would be extremely difficult, if not impossible. The ancient Egyptians were very smart people. Yet they believed in a religion that included the pharaoh himself as a god as well as cats, the sun, and the Nile River. They had one god for the morning, one for midday, one for the evening, and one for nighttime. One had the body of a man and the head of a jackal. One had the body of a woman and the head of a cat. One was one-third lion, one-third zebra, and one-third hippopotamus. I mean, how did they think this stuff up?

The Greeks give us the birth of democracy, Aristotle, and Plato. Doctors still take the Hippocratic oath today, which was originated by Hippocrates over 2,000 years ago. Athens was the intellectual and philosophical center of the world and the foundations for much of our current laws, government and philosophy were drawn from the intellectual leaders of this brilliant era in human history. These were very smart people.

Ancient Rome was splendid in its glory. At its height, the vast Roman Empire stretched over most of the known world. Their road system and aqueducts, built over 2,000 years ago still serve the citizens of modern Rome today. The Coliseum in Rome seated 50,000 (all of whom could quickly and safely exit in just a few minutes because of its design). A retractable canopy roof protected the audience from sun and rain. Below the arena was an extensive tunnel and trapdoor system, which enabled elaborate productions including wild animals of every kind. The Romans also built the Circus Maximus, which held the chariot races and could seat 250,000 people. That compares pretty favorably to the largest stadiums of today. These were very smart people.

Yet the ancient Greeks and Romans practiced polytheism at its best. Each had an elaborate cast of characters with around 50 gods, resembling a television soap opera more than any modern theology. They had a god for every purpose and a purpose for every god. And the gods took sides, often using people like chess pieces in a grand game (everybody wanted to be on the team of Zeus). About 200 B.C. Titus Maccius Platuc said, "The gods play games with men as balls," reflecting on how ancient peoples felt at the mercy of the gods. Now remember, these gods weren't real. People created this pagan ethos and through the centuries, it became part of their belief structure.

In Central and South America the Incas, Mayans and Aztecs created great civilizations. They had vast cities that rivaled the biggest and most advanced cities in Europe at the time including spectacular pyramids. These were very smart people.

While accomplishing all that, they worshipped the sun and practiced human sacrifice. In fact, that was often the purpose of these huge pyramids. In a religious ceremony, on an altar at the very top, they would cut out the heart of the "lucky" person chosen and offer it up to one of their gods. So deep was their belief that it was actually considered an honor to be chosen as the person sacrificed.

The Need Runs Deep

The point here is that advanced civilizations, very accomplished in many ways, held on to religious belief systems that were unsophisticated, unsubstantiated, illogical and in some cases, barbaric. The human need to believe in something is very strong. Humans have been searching for answers as to how things work in this world we live in for eons. The desire for something to believe in, some forces (the gods) to attribute life's mysteries to, runs very deeply in all of us. What we've shown is a ready willingness to invent one in the absence of any evidence we can comprehend.

In the macro sense of each civilization, we see that really smart people have the ability to get some things very right, and some things very wrong, occasionally with dire consequences (as in the case of the Myan who were honored to be selected as human sacrifices to their gods). Most of the things that humans tend to get wrong fall under the umbrella of belief systems.

Much more to the point, and the focus of the rest of this book, is what we believe in our society about success. Even if you believe that the hand of God guides the direction of your life, I'll bet you also believe that He helps those who help themselves and grants you free will and personal responsibility. As a result, a religious perspective has to be integrated with our daily lives and decidedly non-spiritual world. Let's look at what our secular belief system tells us about success.

What We Have Believed About Success

Most people argue that business has become a modern "religion". Yes, we may go to church, but if you examine how we live, money is what we workshop. It could be said that capitalism is the theology and success is heaven here on earth. It does seem that we've lost our way. But in this modern business ethos we believe that hard work and determination are a means of pleasing the "success gods". We practice our "religion" diligently and recite the "liturgy" with heartfelt dedication. As it pertains to the ideas in this book, lots of people (including me for a very long time and probably even you) believe that hard work, passion, motivation and determination will make you successful. We believe that attitude is everything. We believe that we need to be motivated and persistent and set far reaching yet obtainable goals.

I have trained tens of thousands of people from all around the world at our live Internet Mastery workshops and I'm amazed at how similar people's beliefs are as to what it takes to be successful. My informal study clearly indicates that no one fails to achieve success because they are unsure about the attributes of a successful person. Sure, there are some minor variations between people, and their culture, but the basic points are always the same. People refer to getting a good education and getting a job. From there, they'll mention things like hard work, determination, motivation, honesty and integrity. They will include the need to set goals, be passionate and disciplined. The fact of the matter is the well-accepted formula is not complicated—but most people never make it to the turning point of certainty. It's not that people don't know what they're supposed to do or how they're supposed to behave. And for the most part, they follow the prescribed path.

Thousands of books, articles and videos have been made on how to be a "winner" or how to "achieve success", rehashing the same formula over and over, ad infinitum. One Speaker in the seminar business goes as far as saying, "If you are having financial trouble it's because you have the wrong information." There are plenty of people that have achieved financial success in spite of having have the wrong information. There are plenty people that have *not* achieved financial success in spite of having the correct information. Generic statements like this don't do anyone good—except the for the person making the comment. Very few Speakers, Guru's or Experts say very much new, but they are a testament to the insatiable appetite we have for the "keys to success." And now, more than ever, thousands of books, hundreds of millions of likes on Facebook and Instagram and billions of views on YouTube are created each year. We want to believe, and we want to achieve with the belief that the next treatment of the importance of a positive mental attitude will get through to us. Seriously, have you read the book (or seen the movie) "The Secret".

The trouble is some of the brightest, hardest working people I know have never gotten close enough to "the good life" even to catch a whiff of it, let alone spend any considerable amount of time there. This fact is conveniently set aside as the people at the top of the food chain tell those at the bottom to work harder and harder because that's the key to success. Carefully woven into the fabric of our society is the belief in the loosely stated "Law of Compensation". This law states that hard work and dedication will eventually pay off and extremely hard work and intense dedication will pay off big. As long as you believe that, you'll keep working. And we all know that "the only place that success comes before work is in the dictionary." As with other widely accepted belief systems, people are reluctant to propose an alternative.

"If it is to be, it's up to me" is a nice little catch phrase and does remind us of the importance of our intent and determination. It's the omission of influences we can't control and their potential effect on whether "it is to be" that I'm trying to help you understand. The paradox is I'm not suggesting that the traditional approach is wrong, just that it's incomplete. As you'll see later, I encourage, endorse and amplify the core ideas we've all grown up with. I'm simply asserting that a philosophy that also embraces that things happen beyond our control is more complete and more accurate; therefore its better, stronger and more applicable to success—and to our daily lives. When you look at the difference between those that have not achieved a desired level of success and those that ultimately get there, you'll notice the main difference is the way in which they dealt with influences beyond their control.

Random events happen all the time, as do influences in our business we can't control—but are not random. It's not a matter of believing that they do, it's readily apparent that they do. Yet, they've been largely ignored despite the fact that they are part of the fabric of life. I'm not asking that you believe in the effects of outside influences in your business even though they are there. I'm just suggesting that to attribute some events that occur in in life to anything else requires belief. The thinking behind *Outside Influences* springs from evidence, observation and analysis after training tens of thousands of people across planet Earth. These concepts are based on real world interaction, after working with real people who get real results, and not what we want or wish to be so.

Catalytic Concepts

- Our bias to want to believe in something goes back to ancient prehistory.
- Our belief systems are deeply integrated into our view of the world.
- This common wisdom ignores the influence of outside factors and thereby overlooks a major facet of the success equation.

CHAPTER 3
The Attribution Tendency

"Just because a man has gotten from here to all the way over there, doesn't mean he can call you back with directions"
–Will Rogers

One of the most interesting of all human psychological traits is the tendency to attribute a cause and effect relationship. We "work backwards" from an event or circumstance. Restlessly searching for the key to happiness, we look closely at the success of others. We want what they have and we want to do what they do, because this has brought them success.

I believe that becoming the ultimate copycat is one of the most important steps to achieving success. The closer you can follow the system laid out for you the better the chance you will achieve your desired outcome. And yet, sometimes people miss the mark.

Being a copycat means to follow the system exactly as it is shown, without making any changes to it but some people find that task a difficult one. Even when results prove the system works, personal beliefs and the results generated from those beliefs impact the ability to copycat.

On a simple level, you get your car washed and it rains the next day. Now be honest, don't you say, "Do you believe that? Every time I get my car washed it rains." As if the entire weather system of the planet was cognizant of the fact that you got your car washed and reacted accordingly. I've invested in the stock market over the years and I'm always fascinated how the market reacts. It seems almost common place that the moment I buy a stock, it goes down and when I sell that same stock it goes up. Have you ever experienced this? Now, of course we all know these situations are not possible but the internal tendency is undeniable. It's that same psychological tendency that impacts our belief system. Things happen and we want to attribute their occurrence to some cause. We want to understand and we believe things happen for a reason.

We love cause and effect scenarios and "if-then" models, and we relentlessly apply this type of thinking to success when we see it. We conclude that there must be some magic in the approach taken by successful people and we carefully study their perspectives to learn the "secrets" of (their) success. Past attempts to codify the principles of personal success stick to a teachable step-by-step formula. The path to success and the practices engaged in to achieve it are as varied as human beings themselves., not because the system changes but due to the outside influences that occur. Yes, we need a plan that says "A" plus "B" plus "C" will get you results but that plan will still need modification. It's safe to say that most people who reach a high level of success follow a system yet they deal with outside influences differently. In some cases the differences are subtle, in some cases they are dramatic. The key is to understand outside influences are happening and how to deal with them.

I read an article recently that surveyed 1800 people. The results showed that we routinely consider successful people to be smarter, more diligent, more talented and more-worthy than the rest of us. It goes to show you that pre-conceived notions for success run deep in our society. However, if we look at it objectively we will see that the facts don't necessarily support that idea. The desire to discover the "keys to success" is so strong that we overlook the obvious inadequacies and as for help albeit from the wrong people. Sometimes the people who offer the help are the ones who haven't even started yet. Why are we taking advice and input from people who have never done what we want to do and don't have what we want? Because they give us answers that validate our belief system.

As you will soon see, people who've reached high levels of success have unquestionably been positively influenced by outside forces beyond their control. Therefore, any explanation they give of their success will be flawed because unless it takes these forces into consideration. Without knowing any of their personal facts, if I tell you Sharon is very successful, you will draw several conclusions about her intelligence, attitude, work ethic and many other aspects of her character. If I tell you James is not successful, you will come to very different conclusions about him. None of the conclusions you come to will necessarily be accurate about either one of them.

Even with outside influences having an underlying impact on success, it still makes sense to study the lives and thinking and concepts put forth by successful people. When starting a new journey, the last thing you want to do is "try" it on your own. Find a coach or mentor, a person who has made the mistakes before you and who can guide you down the right path. Remember that even though mentors cost more in the short term, mistakes cost far more in the long term. Having the right mentor will include an investment in your future. The important thing to do is be open, grab every idea you can, soak it in and then implement it. Most often it is the seed of an idea that takes root in your mind, draws conceptual nutrients from the reservoir of knowledge and experience coming from coaches and springs forth synergistically. Follow the system and watch for outside influences to appear throughout the journey.

Success Stories

In the seminar business, I see countless success stories that are simply not true. Whether they are actors or simply making up their results is not relevant. We become jaded to the point where people believe that everything said or seen must be fake. I see this all the time at our Internet Mastery preview classes. We host a two-hour event sharing an overview of how to sell on make money on the internet and sell on Amazon. The purpose of the class is enable people who want more information and education to sign up and participate in a 2 ½ day workshop (for a small fee). In this introductory event I routinely show a live "leaderboard" displaying Amazon sales for members of our Internet Mastery Community. Invariably someone will ask if these are real people or if the data is real. Others will overtly say that they know with certainty it can't be real, even though it is very real. I've even had situations where the real person whose real results are shown on the real leaderboard is really in the room—live and in the flesh—and yet people say they must be paid to be there even though their real sales on Amazon (showing up on their real phone from their real Amazon account) match the real leaderboard results.

Knowledge Leads to Success

So much of what we develop as opinion is convention disguised as evaluation. The simple fact is, we're just not always sure what factors create success. But the business works. We know that for certain. And we know how important certain elements are in creating that success.

When people achieve success, honors and accolades are bestowed on them. Some don't like it. Some people prefer to remain anonymous because they don't want others to see how successful they really are. In addition to satisfying the desire of the curious "wannabes" to learn the secrets of success, successful people must deal with a far more powerful internal need. The personal need for the justification of their success and its accompanying abundance is compelling. It's well documented that, deep in their hearts, many people who achieve success had an underlying sense of self-doubt when they started. They confess they did not necessarily believe they would succeed but moved forward anyway. And now, they are unstoppable.

If we can't fully analyze success, there must be factors beyond our comprehension that influence it. I want to re-emphasize that hard work, determination, and all of the traits we've all known and talked about for so many years do play a significant role when people achieve success. While knowledge and acumen do matter, taking action is a key element to the people who achieve success. Moving forward. Going all in. Taking a leap. Jumping.

Casino Connections

Knowing how to gamble (or "how to" just about anything else) doesn't guarantee success. Surely gambling is random; everybody knows that. Now, I've spent a fair amount of time in a casino, watching my parents and then participating myself from time to time. Certainly it's a very interesting opportunity to study people, for sure.

Now the ideas of attribution and outside influences come up all the time as you're watching people in a casino. I enjoy playing blackjack and roulette. My dad was a big fan of blackjack and my mom loved roulette. Both are fun, but roulette can be very exciting and if you get lucky you can win a lot of money with odds of 35 to 1 if you hit a number directly. Now I've watched the game enough to recognized that there really is no such thing as the law of averages as it relates to any single spin. In other words, the ball and the wheel are not sentient and they are not aware of what number came out on the last spin. Furthermore, they're not aware of what number came out over the last 100 spins. And they certainly don't know what numbers the players are betting on. So in that regard, each individual spin is a separate event unto itself.

Interestingly, and somewhat paradoxically, over the course of thousands of spins, the law of averages does hold true. This tends to come up if you've been playing a while and perhaps betting on one particular number, or set of numbers, to come out. There are 38 numbers on an American roulette wheel. If you're playing eight numbers consistently, one of them should come out roughly every five spins. Now I have watched my mom play roulette for hours without one of her favorite eight numbers coming out. This is over the course of a couple of hundred spins. In that short interval, the law of averages doesn't necessarily work. But, human nature being what it is, if a particular number hasn't come out for a while you might get a "hunch" that it's about to happen. Sometimes when that would happen, my mom would increase her bet.

The funny thing is, if a number comes out and you had a hunch that it would, you would be likely to exclaim (as I have seen my mom do many times) "I KNEW that number was going to come out!" Now obviously, she didn't actually know; if she really knew she would have bet the table maximum on the number and would not have bet on any other numbers. But at that particular point she had a hunch and it paid off. Sometimes they do and sometimes they don't. More often than not at the casino, they don't.

Where this all gets particularly interesting is watching the other people at the table. If you happen to have a string of numbers in a row that come out right, you'll start to take on a certain posture. You'll start to seem like you really know the game (event if you've never previously played). You'll start to act like you really know what's going on. It's impossible for this not to affect how you think and act. And amazingly, the other people around the table will start to defer to you. You'll hear them say things like, "Hey follow that guy, he knows what he is doing." They'll be amazed at your winnings and they'll move their hand out of the way when you place a bet. This all happens because they're attributing to you an understanding of how to win at roulette because the evidence seems to indicate that you do. Other times, when luck is not going your way you get pretty stupid, pretty fast. People around the table figure you are new to the game and start offering advice on how to bet.

Attribution applies to many other aspects of life. For instance, have you ever talked to someone who's lost a lot of weight? Someone who's lost a lot of weight suddenly has the knowledge of a Ph.D. in nutrition. They lecture others on the way to lose weight and what the other people are doing wrong. They explain how the body metabolizes food. They explain the proper way to combine different food groups. They know when you're supposed to eat and when you're not supposed to eat. They might event write an eBook on the subject. How is it that they know all of these things—well they must know because they've lost a lot of weight.

Have you noticed how many 25 year-old life coaches there are on social media?

In virtually any human endeavor, people who do well at something, who succeed at it are automatically elevated. Now, I'm not saying they shouldn't be. Certainly, we can learn from virtually everyone. I just want people to be aware of this propensity toward attribution, which simply is not always appropriate or correct.

The game of roulette is a simple game. There are only a few options. The rules are clearly spelled out and as long as you assume that the casinos are honest, all of the related factors in the game are obvious and apparent to all the participants. Life on the other hand, does not practice full disclosure. Success in life or in any business is many, many times more complicated than playing roulette at the casino. There are thousands, perhaps hundreds of thousands of variables so we must be very careful when attributing success to certain factors.

Success is Evasive

While my overall bias about people is good, I readily acknowledge that some people really don't want success as badly as they say they do or aren't willing to pay the price for it. Their lack of effort, lack of initiative, or lack of talent has landed them in a place where they have little good going on in their lives. But we all know people for whom life has not given up its bounty who do struggle, who "shouldn't be" where they are. I'm talking about solid people who are smart, diligent, and have all of the tools that should have resulted in massive success but for some reason it has eluded them. Now the old common wisdom they did something (or didn't do something) that ended up derailing their career or business comes to mind. In other words, it's their fault they didn't make it big. They're somehow inherently less worthy than the CEO's of the world.

Consider this passage from *Conned Again, Watson!*, (2002, Perseus Books Group, page 21) a book by Colin Bruce, a physicist and science writer living in Oxford. He wrote popular *The Einstein Paradox and Other Science Mysteries Solved by Sherlock Holmes*, in which the solutions to Sherlock Holmes cases are based on apparent paradoxes. We find Watson and Holmes in their Baker Street apartment on the evening of the last day of 1899. Holmes is in a philosophical mood and remarks to Watson that while they can look forward to the New Year with hopefulness and the anticipation of continuing prosperity, others can only look forward to more debt and despair. Watson replies that those with little can only blame their own "idleness" and "folly." Holmes then offers the following analysis.

"Once I might have said so, Watson. But the more I see of life, the more I am struck by how great a part is played not by brains, or skill, or character, but by simply chance. The success or failure of a business venture, or a marriage, or a war, can depend more on the blind roll of Fate's dice than on any planning. Life is a chaotic business, and the most unpredictable of happenings can determine the fate of one man's life or of a whole nation. The whim of Lady Luck rules all.

I think Holmes (Bruce) might have gone a little too far there, but the interchange does show, via Watson's comments, our tendency to make assumptions about people who don't reach high levels of success. Somehow, it's easy for me to see Sherlock Holmes coming to a different perspective than the status quo.

To be clear, I believe it's impossible to have a successful business unless you first acquire some degree of specific knowledge, then have the courage to take the risk and start it. Plus, you have to work hard, have a great product, treat people fairly, work with a mentor and do a few others things right along the way. All of that is a prerequisite; without it, you're not even in the game and you don't have a business in the first place. But you still need a great deal of cooperation from influences beyond your control, and sometimes in the beginning, beyond your comprehension for your business to soar. And if things are not turning out the way you had hoped, that does not necessarily mean you are doing, or have done, anything wrong. Outside influences may have created circumstances that are aligned against you and all of the hard work in the world is not going to overcome that.

For many people, this is a liberating idea. The logic within the material in this book shuns attribution for a lot of reasons. When something bad happens, the common pattern of thought is to labor with guilt or search for answers as to "Why?". Once you understand outside influences you'll see that there doesn't always need to be a "Why"; there just "Is". The truth is, "Stuff happens". Most of the time there's no rhyme or reason to it, but for eons mankind has tried in vain to find the causes of life's terrible events. Likewise, when good things occur, we make connections that really aren't there. The pitfall with attribution is the very real possibility of false attribution.

The simple fact is that the old formulas just don't work all of the time. They appear to work some of the time, and that perpetuates them. Furthermore, they serve our organizations well because they keep people motivated and focused on hard work. For the majority of people, there is a huge contradiction between what we are told will happen if we follow the rules and what actually occurs.

This contraction is hard for people to process because the old framework left no room for the consideration of outside influences. Therefore, if a person had not achieved a high degree of success, they must be deficient in some way.

Further complicating matters, we all know successful people who are not that bright, that don't even work all that hard, but have achieved a high degree of success (in a lot of cases, the hard work that successful people do is designed to justify the success they're having). In other words, they don't follow the rules and end up in a better place, and this is not uncommon. Sometimes after meeting or interacting with a highly successful person you might find yourself asking, "How in the world did he or she get there?" There just doesn't seem to always be a correlation between people's overall talent and ability and where they end up in life. And yet, understanding outside influences can have an impact on your ultimate success.

 Catalytic Concepts

- There is a strong human desire to understand the causes for all of the phenomena we observe around us. We believe in cause and effect and we don't like loose ends. We like for things to add up.
- Social Media plays on and reinforces attribution in our society.
- We believe we know the "causes" of success to be hard work, education, dedication and many other noble human traits. We tent to attribute them to people who are successful.
- Successful people are not always fully aware of the factors that have led to their success.
- We tend to view the ideas and opinions of less successful people with skepticism, but good ideas can come from anyone. All people have valuable insights to offer.

CHAPTER 4

Doublethink

"Doublethink means the power of holding two contradictory beliefs in one's mind simultaneously, and accepting both of them."
–George Orwell

A Useful Mental Tool

Expansive flexible thinking has the ability to believe / hold true two seemingly contradictory ideas at the same time. This is very useful to us because life is full of contractions and mysteries. We have heard the well-known observation, "The more things change, the more they remain the same," and yet in this situation we can easily process and understand the differences despite the apparent contradiction. We know that things don't always add up exactly, and that's okay. We often have to engage doublethink as we confront new ideas and thinking.

Consider the words of one of the great thinkers of the twentieth century, Dr. Carl Sagan: "It seems to me what is called for is an exquisite balance between two conflicting needs; the most skeptical scrutiny of all hypotheses that are served up to us and at the same time a great openness to new ideas. If you are only skeptical, then no new ideas make it through to you. You never learn anything new. You become a crotchety old person convinced that nonsense rules the world (with much data to support your theories). On the other hand, if you are open to the point of gullibility and have not an ounce of skeptical sense in you, then you cannot distinguish useful ideas from the worthless ones. If all ideas have equal validity then you are lost, because then, it seems to me, no ideas have any validity, at all." (The Burden of Skepticism," Pasadena Lecture, 1987).

This "exquisite balance" helps us get our mental arms around big ideas, which often contain elements of contradiction within them. We can see the wisdom of the old saying "Fools rush in where angels fear to tread." Yeah, that makes sense. "Haste makes waste," you know. But then again, "He who hesitates is lost" and "Opportunities don't go away, they just go to someone else." Both ideas can be accepted in our mind and it is understood that the situation can dictate where we should "make haste" or step back for more analysis.

The message of this book is not that all of what we've learned about life and success in the past is wrong—far from it. The changes I'm suggesting are pretty subtle, actually. Perhaps more importantly, they must be embraced along with the more traditional ideas of success despite the fact that, on the surface, they may seem to contradict one another.

There are two facets of a successful life. There's the proactive side; our initiative, motivation, hard work and determination. I acknowledge the role we play in affecting the ultimate outcome of our lives as a dominant factor. I reiterate this to be certain it comes through loud and clear. But what I'm suggesting is that there might be a new and different facet; factors beyond our control also play a role. Sometimes they provide a defining moment. What I'd like you to understand is how to blend these two ideas and develop a framework for moving forward that acknowledges and accepts both. So, to really "get it' you've got to have your mind opened wide enough to embrace all the other ideas and theories, even if they seem to contradict each other or the things you believe. You've got to use doublethink.

The Yin and Yang

In China, the early Han dynasty (207B.C.-9 A.D.) devoted itself to blending the many schools of thought that existed in ancient Eastern philosophy. This synergistic approach, known as the "Han Synthesis", was the origin of the concept of yin-yang.

As the ancient Chinese philosophers saw it, the Yin and the Yang represented the two opposite yet complimentary forces or principles that make up all aspects and phenomena of life. They saw "contradiction" everywhere and recognized the need for forces in life to have counter-balancing factors. They developed an incredible way to represent and think about the important concept of balance.

Yin is earth, female, dark, passive, and absorbing; it is present in even numbers, valleys and streams, and is represented by the tiger, the color orange, and a broken line. Yang is heaven, male, light, active and penetrating; it is present in odd numbers and mountains, and is represented by the dragon, the color azure and an unbroken line. Together they represent the interdependence of opposites.

The ancient Eastern philosophers and thinkers understood quite well the importance of this kind of mental agility. They extended the entire universe the harmony of contradicting ideas. Wisdom dictates that no concept is singular unto itself, and it's reassuring that this was clear thousands of years ago. For example, we may have a strong sense of urgency, anxious for success, wanting to enjoy the bounty now, right away. But we must also be patient about the journey, understanding that it takes time to achieve excellence.

Using the extreme opposite colors of black and white, swirling together, harmoniously coexisting within the perfect circle, each with a "heart" of the other, showing that contradictory points of view often carry with them a seed of their opposite.

Maturity Means Gray

As we mature we leave the world where everything is black and white and move to a world dominated by shades of gray. This is not because we lose the passion of our youth. It's because experience confronts us with overwhelming evidence that things are not always as they appear. We become suspect of the "knowledge" of others because we've come to understand that "reality" is different for different people. It's not reality, but perception of that reality that actually guides us. Acquiring new ideas and information can be like pulling a giant fishing net from the sea. A wide variety and quality of data must be brought in for consideration, some of them useful and valid, some not.

Sometimes we draw conclusions based on irrelevant experiences and misconstrued evidence. As we evolve and grow, we come to understand this about all human beings, even ourselves, so we leave room for it as we construct our beliefs and even our "knowledge". For most people, our perception is our reality ("I think therefore I am").

There was an interesting study conducted by a professor at Yale Law School that highlighted the flaws that can be present even in what we witness first hand. As she taught approximately 100 students in a lecture hall, the teacher noticed a wide-eyed man, in kind of a daze, wander into the room via the front door about 20 feet to the right of her. He just stood there for a second and looked around. The professor ignored him and at first continued to lecture. The man then started to walk toward her. She interrupted her speech and ask him what he wanted. He continued to walk toward her, and suddenly grabbed her purse that was sitting on the table next to the podium. He turned and bolted out the door in a flash. The students were stunned. They gasped and a couple of the male students started after him but were stopped at the door by the professor's assistant.

The "crime" had been staged—the entire incident on video—with every detail of what happened recorded. Now the fun began as, one by one, the students were taken out of the room and questioned about what they saw. Remember, these were bright young people who were paying attention, focused on the front of the room. Well, it was amazing to hear their "testimony" as they each recounted what they saw.

What did he have on? A blue shirt, a green sweater, a brown jacket… their answers were all over the place. He was 5'7" to 6'4" tall and weighed anywhere from 145 lbs. to 230 lbs. Did he have a hat? Why color were his shoes. Brown was the majority answer. The room was split. The moral of the story is that eye witness testimony can be far from accurate.

In addition to the question of the veracity of what we see, there's also the phenomenon of our own internal editing. One of the wonderful things about human memory is that accuracy is optional. What we remember with certainty occasionally has "corrupt" files. Sometimes we just forget, but think we remember. Other times our subconscious mind makes a few little adjustments just to help everything fit together nice and neat. Perhaps you've had the experience of holding a particular memory in one fashion, only to find irrefutable evidence to the contrary. And people are so funny about this—when it happens we say, "Well, I guess based on the evidence, I didn't have that quite correct, but I've got the rest of it right for sure." Oh really?

"Knowledge" is Suspect

It makes good sense to take just about everything with a grain of salt. The body of human knowledge is in a constant state of metamorphosis. Thomas Edison once said, "We don't know one tenth of one percent about anything." The statement highlights mankind's general ignorance showing that what we "know" today we may find to be somewhat different tomorrow. This is true even in scientific fields of study and it's true in our unscientific day-to-day lives. And this doesn't even factor in duplicity or ulterior motives, which unfortunately, are very much a part of interpersonal communications especially in business. But setting that point aside, you must understand that being honest is not the same as being correct. It's very possible for a person to make an honest mistake and think something happened (or that it happened in a certain way) when it didn't.

If you have ever been part of an event that was covered in the media you've witnessed this phenomenon. For example, we read an online article or newsfeed to be informed, to learn what is happening in the world. I've had occasion through the years to have intimate knowledge of circumstances or events that have some notoriety to them and subsequently read a published account online. It's unnerving in a way, because virtually every time, they get some aspects of the event wrong. And when you extrapolate out you really begin to suspect the accuracy of the media.

To further prove the point, spend an afternoon in front of the TV, switching the channel every fifteen minutes between CNN and Fox News. You might think you have multiple personality disorder.

Napoleon highlighted this when he said, "History is a fable people agree to believe."

According to President Trump, most news is "Fake News"—of course, that's how he describes the news he doesn't agree with.

Modes of Thinking

Psychologists have identified essentially two modes or approaches to thinking how we relate to new ideas:

Mode 1—Reason precedes sentiment (the rare mode)

This unfortunately is the most uncommon mode of thinking. In this mode, people, in the process of forming an opinion, examine carefully all of the facts of the matter, form a hypothesis, and then attempt to disprove their own hypothesis. After a certain amount of rigorous examination and refutation of their own hypothesis, they may or may not conclude that the hypothesis is sound. If the hypothesis does not survive close examination and scrutiny, it is discarded and a new hypothesis is formed. If the hypothesis is sound, it is incorporated into their view of the world.

In the process of incorporating the hypothesis or idea into our world view, certain sentiments are attached to the idea... the idea becomes a "belief". It is the hallmark of the rational mind to allow reason to justify sentiment. Once we decide on a rational, reasoned hypothesis, we develop a sentiment to support and strengthen it. Reason precedes sentiment... reason justifies sentiment.

Mode 2—Sentiment precedes reason (the ubiquitous mode)

This is by far, the most common form of thinking; we encounter it all the time in dealing with others. In this mode of thinking, a sentiment exists first, and then hypotheses are formed to "rationalize" the sentiment. The individual seeks facts and ideas that justify the sentiment... sentiment is justified by facts and reason. This is an inferior and immature form of thinking but unfortunately, it's wide-spread.

Consider this—people surround themselves with people who are of like mind, people who have similar beliefs, and a similar outlook. We "seek out" people who will validate our beliefs, good or bad. This is why people will go to different Doctor's appointments until they get the answer they are looking for.

Cognitive Dissonance

Cognitive Dissonance Theory, developed by Leon Festinger (1957), is concerned with the relationship amongst our thoughts. It's all part of that wonderful enigma we call human consciousness. A cognition may be thought of as a piece of knowledge, a perception or a belief. People hold a multitude of cognitions simultaneously, and these cognitions form irrelevant, consonant or dissonant relationships with one another.

Cognitive irrelevance describes the bulk of the relationships among a person's cognitions. Irrelevance simply means that the two cognitions have nothing to do with each other. We know that Washington, DC is the capital of the United States and we know that the grass is green. These two thoughts have no relevance to each other as most ideas in our mind do not, and that's all fine.

Two cognitions are consonant if one cognition follows from, or fits with, the other. People like consonance among their cognitions. We do not know whether this stems from the nature of the human organism or whether it is learned during the process of socialization, but people appear to prefer cognitions that fit together to those that do not. We like it when things add up and fit together. Mary is bright and a hard worker. Mary is very successful in her career. That just feels right. That's consonance... it flows.

Two cognitions are said to be dissonant if one follows from the opposite of the other. What happens to people when they discover dissonant cognitions? The answer to this question forms the basic postulate of *Festinger's Theory*. A person who has dissonant or discrepant cognitions is said to be in a state of psychological dissonance, which is experienced as unpleasant psychological tension. This tension state has drive-like properties that are much like those of hunger and thirst. When things don't add up in our mind, we search for ways to discount or disprove the ideas that are dissonant.

When someone doesn't have the money to invest in education, software, a business or themselves, they look for reasons to blame the system (therefore validating why they can't or won't get involved.)

To protect against dissonance, we discount and outright reject ideas that don't conform to our worldview. People will vigorously defend their beliefs and sometimes things can get quite heated. In other words, people can be close minded and stubborn. I'm sure you already know that.

We just don't like it when things don't add up or don't conform to our beliefs. It really can produce an uncomfortable feeling. Consider this: Mark is bright and a hard worker. Mark's career is on the rocks and he's going nowhere. Those cognitions are dissonant for most of us and we quickly begin to doubt the veracity of the assessment of Mark's intellect and work ethic.

Cognitive dissonance will cause you to reject or at least overlook or modify information that is not consistent with your view of the world. This makes it very difficult to grow and be open to new perspectives. Have you ever been involved in a conversation with someone where they just won't listen to reason? Have you ever seen people resist overwhelming logic? (Those are rhetorical questions of course). You're seeing cognitive dissonance in action. The new idea just can't compute for them. It's too illogical to be logical.

It also makes us readily open to ideas that support what we already believe. Consonant ideas that fit with what "know" and accept are readily welcomed into our minds and find fertile soil. It is like intellectual segregation where we welcome that which is consistent with the ideas that already "live in the neighborhood", but watch out when a different idea tries to move in.

Fitting Outside Influences In

As it relates to the central theme of this book, you must suspend cognitive dissonance and stretch open your mind to accept the idea that outside influences play an important part in determining the outcome of your life. Accepting and understanding this, we must reconcile it with the fact that you must also work extremely hard to achieve success. You must work smart and strive to be effective. You must care about the people in your life and the people you work with. You must manage your money and your time well. And you must become very good at what you do. And you must allow a mentor or coach to guide you in the process. Unless you do all of those things your chances for big-time success are very low. On the one hand, we accept and realize that a certain influence is exerted on us by factors outside of our control, but we also know that we are the single largest determinant and we do have a great deal of power to put the odds in our favor for success.

It's simplistic to think that life can be reduced to neat compact "boxes" of ideas that all fit together beautifully without intellectual conflict.

Recently a respected author and speaker said this of their new book: "My goal with this book is simple: Deliver a formula that anyone, anywhere in the world can use to finally shape themselves into a successful Entrepreneur." Or how about this one: "Within weeks of reading this book, (so and so) became an instant success." If only that was true.

Experience teaches us that there can be more to a situation than meets the eye. Controlled stress in the structure of a building or a bridge makes it stronger and more stable—able to withstand pressure and force and support a load. Crossbeams pull while girders push. The tension creates strength. Our minds work the same way. The tension of apparently conflicting concepts strengthens our point of view. As we tighten down on the ideas of self-determination, our understanding of outside influences prevents a conceptual implosion and makes for a much stronger outlook and framework for interpreting the world around us.

Catalytic Concepts

- We need an "exquisite balance" to allow us to believe two seemingly contradictory ideas simultaneously

- The ancient Chinese philosopher of Yin and Yang helps enlighten us regarding this idea and shows that man has considered the harmony in conflict for eons.
- What we "know" to be true is drawn from our perceptions and we must accept that our knowledge and our memories may be slightly flawed.
- The central concept of *Outside Influences* contains contradiction to the casual observer: It accepts that we are the primary factors in determining the course of our lives, but it also acknowledges that forces outside of our control also influence our lives, sometimes greatly. Without accepting outside influences, the formula is incomplete.
- There is an intellectual strength and integrity that comes from the competing forces of conflicting ideas
- Blending these concepts and accepting them into our framework for understanding how the world works gives us a stronger overall philosophical foundation.

CHAPTER 5

The Law of Outside Influences

"The truth that makes men free is for the most part the truth which men prefer not to hear."

–Herbert Sebastian Agar

Omnipresent Yet Often Unseen

O utside influences, what occurs beyond our control, have a significant effect on the direction and outcome of our lives. You know that now. You should believe that now.

In addition to our own efforts as we've discussed, knowledge, skills and attitudes, all of which are very important, a multitude of factors outsides of ourselves, beyond our control (and often beyond our comprehension or awareness) exert a tremendous amount of influence on our lives. It is the combined effect of our internal dynamics and outside influences that determines what we accomplish and ultimately our success. There is a complex, interdependent relationship between the decisions we make and actions we take and these innumerable outside influences. Their efforts can be profound or subtle, positive or negative. Furthermore, when you examine your life in its totality, you'll observe that "in front of" every key event in our lives is a series of perhaps thousands of random events as well as actual decisions and actions, some of our own, some of others, that enabled or created that moment, without which, the event itself would probably never have occurred.

Now, you can choose to ignore this concept, as you have probably been doing (which of course doesn't make it go away). Or you can embrace it, study it, and become more aware of this aspect of the brilliant elegant system we call life. When you open up to the idea, you will see that outside influences are more pervasive in your world than you would have imagined. The more cognizant you become the more you'll see the interdependence and relevance of the outside influences with day-to-day events in your life. Or you can continue to rely on complex belief structures to rationalize and explain the events of your life and the world.

For eons humans have constructed complicated belief systems to try to explain the many manifestations of outside influences in our lives. Centuries ago (around 1325 A.D.) a brilliant mathematician and philosopher by the name of William Ockham developed an approach to problem solving that I have found to be a very useful tool. It cut (no pun intended) right to the heart of the matter and has come to be known as "Ockham's Razor." Concisely said, Ockham reasoned that *"the simplest theory that fits the facts of a problem is most likely the correct theory."*

If we apply Ockham's Razor to some of the key questions of life, the simplest theory is that much of life is random. No specific plan, no destiny; just beautifully, exquisitely, simply… random.

As we search for reasons "why" things occur we can benefit from understanding that the world functions as a gracefully balanced system, and that system is dynamic and in a constant state of evolution and change. As a result, events occur, circumstances flow into and out existence, and outside influences and random events all come into play for all of us. This is not something to be feared. The world has no ulterior motives. That's the awesome intrigue of it, watching it unfold and observing the connections, coincidences, opportunities and situations that emerge. It may seem natural to be afraid of the unknown but the appropriate response is to embrace it with wonder not to build false bridges to a hypothetical tomorrow. It's okay to acknowledge that, to an extent, life happens to us.

Mokita

In New Guinea they have a word, *mokita*. It's said to mean "truth we all know, but agree not to talk about it." To me, the idea of outside influences is a mokita. It's so obvious (granted I've been thinking about it for a long time) and so important, yet it has not made its way into the general consciousness or dialogue. It's my hope it will as millions of people read this book. To a large degree, deep down in our hearts, we've always known that outside influences were factors in the equation. It's taboo to talk about but everyone understands the implicitly, successful people can attribute a percentage of their success to being "lucky". A few people get some really bad breaks along the way and most of us end up somewhere in the middle. But it seems to me that no one has thought through what the implications of this are for the commonly accepted principles of success.

One friend of mine, a speaker in the seminar business, read an early draft of Outside Influences for me. He said he found it liberating and refreshing to openly talk about and think about something that this business made it impossible to acknowledge or discuss.

I've looked closely at the idea of outside influences because I see so many benefits to individuals and to society at large from acknowledging its presence and effect. I think for the most part it's simply misunderstood. Misunderstanding comes from ignorance. Ignorance tends to manifest itself in limiting, fearful behavior.

Oversimplification is a primary factor in causing the misunderstanding. It is not accurate simply to just say, "Successful people are lucky." We all know it takes a lot more than just luck. If you want success you must be willing to work your tail off. And then, in addition, for you to reach the heights, outside influences have to come to your aid. When all of the factors come together, you have the "Perfect Storm" of success. But remember, the perfect storm at sea, as in the movies and as in life, comes along only once in a great while.

Likewise, it's not fair to say of someone who doesn't reach high levels of success that they are lazy, stupid, malcontents or failures. That's a common misconception. It's also quite likely that outside influences have come to bear on their situation to create a negative rather than positive circumstance. I'm not saying that people don't make bad decisions along the way, we do. But many factors go into the mix that sets the direction of our lives.

Another possibility as to why this way of thinking has not come to the forefront in the past is the very narrow, limiting way people have thought about an extremely complicated subject. We want to understand. We want to feel in control. We want to think that if we do this, that will happen. So, we block out the evidence of outside influences and focus on the understandable and controllable. Or we put it in the hands of the mystical and abdicate responsibility altogether (let me read my horoscope and see what's going to happen to me today).

It's the combination of both internal factors and outside influences that determines the events in our lives (remember doublethink). This is especially true when the results are at the extreme ends of the spectrum of success and failure.

Some are afraid to acknowledge this for fear of providing an excuse for people who don't reach their goals. This is out of genuine concern for them and for society. Though well founded, that concern is ill conceived. It's been my experience in life that ignoring something doesn't make it go away. A person who doesn't brush their teeth will have bad breath. Ignoring poor dental hygiene and bad breath doesn't make it go away. The personal strategy that results from understanding the effects of outside influences is not to sit back and relax and wait for your ship to come in (or for your breath to smell better)—far from it. As you'll see later, the strategy is in fact to swim out and greet every ship you can, to see if that's your ship. Accepting and working to understand this will put a person in a much better position reach success. Outside influences is the missing piece to completing the success puzzle.

There's another part of all of this that we really do have to examine. Successful people for the most part do not like to talk about the effects of outside influences. They are very engrossed in convincing themselves and others that they are more-worthy than everybody else. It's been said that every self-made man worships his creator. False pride sometimes lets the wealthy look down on the less fortunate. "They don't try as hard. They don't set goals. They are not as smart or as well educated. They are not motivated." The last thing they want to hear is that in some ways "the system" has bestowed abundance on them. They're much more prone to, and comfortable with, statements like, "The harder I work, the luckier I get," the implication being that the hard work is the key to success and corollary to it, that people who are not lucky are not hard workers. Hmmmm… gotta think about that one.

I'm all for hard work and consider it a prerequisite for success but I know an awful lot of hard working people who still have trouble making ends meet at the end of the month.

Our mokita has been the success paradigm and its lack of consistent performance. In *Outside Influences,* I'm suggesting that we take it out, examine it thoroughly, discuss its merits, and add the influences of factors beyond our control to the mix. Perhaps you have a mokita in your business (or you may have a few). You may want to try the same penetrating approach. You may find a better way, an improvement that makes a marked difference.

The Loser's Limp

People who have not yet reached the summit refrain from making the point of the effects of outside influences because that would be seen as making excuses (sour grapes). One motivational speaker calls it a "loser's limp"… an excuse for poor performance. The effects of things outside of your control are very real and to ignore them and push on can have dire consequences and yet they happen more frequently than we want to admit.

Recently I was hosting a mastermind session with a group of Internet Mastery Community Protégé students. The subject was "product sourcing strategies for the holidays".

As early as I can remember, I learned not make excuses in business for my lack of results. In fact, I was taught that the only thing that mattered was performance and that excuses had no place in business (or in life for that matter). I've learned that this isn't necessarily true, but here's an example that challenged my thinking.

The best-selling products during the online holiday season are items in the toy category. And, many of my students who sell on Amazon utilize a strategy called "Arbitrage"; buying a product in one marketplace on clearance or closeout and selling it in another marketplace for a profit. The best place to "Arbitrage" toys to sell on Amazon was to buy them from Toys R Us.

Outside influences in macro proportions can negatively impact your business if you aren't aware of what's happening around you. In this specific case, Toys R Us has gone out of business in the US and in the UK. Toys R Us is still thriving in Canada.

In the mastermind, attendees began to make excuses as to how they would no longer be able to make money, how this was the worst thing that could ever happen to them and how sales were going to be awful this holiday season without realizing how powerful an opportunity this situation really is for the people who take maximum advantage of it.

Once Toys R Us closed, there wasn't anything they could do about it. It was completely out of their control. I explained the concept of the "Losers Limp." I talked about excuses and how they can hold us back.

Once they realized the significance of the opportunity—that less people would have access to the same toys, that wholesalers were looking for more vendors, that there would be less competition, and that the opportunity was better for the people who "see it", they began to get focused on the right outcome.

Instead of focusing on a negative situation that we had no control over, instead of making excuses, we redirected our attention to how to build and grow a business with strategies and insights ignored by most people. We moved towards optimum success rather than blaming a situation we can't control for our lack of results.

The fact of the matter is that we are seldom at optimum performance level. Jean Giraudoux, the French dramatist, said, "Only the mediocre are always at their best." One of the keys to success is learning to operate on a long-term basis just one gear down from top gear. Reserve that top gear for certain premier opportunities. Understand that occasionally outside influences will prevent you from being at your optimum and then work through it. It's also possible that they could be influencing the performance of your competition. Never take winning for granted. Remember, the "loser's limp" could very well be real, but hopefully just a temporary, limitation on someone's performance.

Personal Responsibility

Accepting personal responsibility for your life and its outcome is necessary for success. Without doublethink, people are fearful of "letting in" the idea of outside influences because they think it would mean abdicating personal responsibility. They fear that outside influences suggests life happens to us without our input. That is not what I'm saying at all.

To become successful, you must be prepared to work very hard, obviously. You must cross all the t's and dot all the i's and then maybe, just maybe things will come out your way. I'm not saying that outside factors totally determine the outcome of our lives. I'm saying they influence it. But there's also a host of other factors well within your control whose combined effect has the greatest influence on who you are and where you end up in this world.

The bottom line on personal responsibility is simple; you are completely responsible for how you live your life. Whether you end up among the highly successful or not will be determined in part by that, and in part by outside influences. And in the long run, it's the former not the latter that really matters anyway. It's how we act in the "moments of truth" that we face. It's how we treat those we love and those we work with. It's about staying true to oneself and one's ideals. All of those are within our control and we have a responsibility to ourselves to manifest the good within us. To paraphrase the ancient wisdom, what good is it to make a lot of money if you must compromise who you are or subjugate your principles? People who do that are suffering from a bad case of mistaken identity. They have identified the wrong goals in life and as a result, lead a life that is warped and unfulfilling.

The Sources of Outside Influences

There are three different kinds of influences beyond our selves and the things we control that can and affect our lives on a regular basis.

1. Random Events

Random events are occurrences with no identifiable reason for the to happen at a particular moment. You're in a hurry to get somewhere and a little old lady in a 1979 Honda Civic pulls out right in front of you going 10 mph below the speed limit on a winding two lane road. I'm going to talk about "Random Events Theory" a little later in this chapter but I want to identify and distinguish random events from other outside influences. Many things happen in life, and in business, that are random and unexplainable. No matter how hard you look you cannot completely identify or fully explain why and how they occur. The old lady could have just as easily gotten to the intersection 5 seconds later and you would have been long gone. The weather, in any particular place, on any particular day is random (although many of us do control where we live and can therefore choose the climate we prefer) and has a way of reminding us of Mother Nature's more playful side from time to time.

2. Actions and Decisions of People Outside of Our Sphere of Influence

Right at this moment, as you read this sentence, someone that you don't even know, and certainly never met, could be making a decision or taking an action that will affect your life. Different from random events, these outside influences are a result of things that other people do. Our "sphere of influence" is our personal world, the people, places, and things we interact with, the organizations we are a part of, the facets of our lives we engage with each day. Beyond that relatively tight circle is a whole world that we are connected to.

At any point in time, President Donald Trump and Russian President Vladimir Putin (whom I will conclude you have not met) could be making decisions and taking actions that could literally affect the direction of world history. There are many other people who we do not know that could intrude on our lives in some way. China could see an increase in trade taxes and duties imposed on key materials, resulting in an increase in prices or goods. Someone could be digging a pool in your neighborhood and hit a water main or power line near your house. Someone you're counting on may drop the ball, leaving you high and dry. On the plus side, new technologies could emerge that could positively revolutionize your business. Air BNB and Uber did this for entire industries.

We want to reach out, expand our knowledge and understanding of the world around us, as well we should. Knowledge is power and power lets us exert influence. We want to know what is going on. But a minnow has a better chance of swallowing a whale than we have of grasping all the of the widespread factors that affects our lives and our careers. It's a massive and complex system with vast connections and implications.

3. Actions and Decisions of People Within Our Sphere of Influence

Within our sphere of familiarity, people we know are making decisions and taking actions all the time. Throughout our childhood, we rely on our parents' judgment but we are also subject to their circumstances. There's many a person who grew up in a particular town because their dad was transferred there and that became a defining decision for their development as children. If you look at people's lives closely you will see a great deal of randomness comes into play in life circumstances, and decisions play off those factors. Each day, many known and unknown actions and decisions of others influence us. What is your number one competitor thinking and planning? People get jobs through personal introductions. Couples meet and fall in love as a result of age-old friendly matchmaking activities including online dating. What does your boss have on his or her agenda? What is your top salesperson contemplating? What about the owners of the company you work for? Did you know your neighbor was planning a big graduation party for his son this spring? Actions taken by those within our "sphere of influence" affect our lives to one degree or another. Things that happen in the lives of those we love impact us directly, yet we seldom have any ability to influence them. To paraphrase John Donne, no one is an island.

The sources of outside influences can be completely random, or the result of actions and / or decisions made by others, some of whom we know and some we do not.

The Scope of Outside Influences

Outside influences affect our lives on five different levels:

1. Massive Macro Influences:

These are big, powerful, socio-economic forces that influence all of us. They are major, political, systemic, global or national, identifiable factors such as the economy, a Supreme Court nominee or a presidential election. These happen all around us and are we generally aware of them. For the most part, we tend to ignore them until they confront us with change, negative or positive. Who is in White House impacts us. The Prime Interest Rate impacts us. Social unrest impacts us.

Some outside influences are obvious and not arguable. The economy affects all of us although it can sometimes be difficult to understand exactly how. The economy is so large and so complex today, influenced greatly by global considerations, that even the brightest economists don't agree on its direction. For us as individuals, it is hard to ascertain its direct effect, but most people would readily acknowledge it can and does affect most businesses and therefore more careers. In some cases, the effect can be spectacular and in some cases, it can cause ruin. And the economy is merely one of the influential factors along the way over which we have no control. Furthermore, certain businesses can actually thrive in a "bad" economy and individuals can reap huge rewards when the stock market crashes.

Social trends can influence the success of a business or a person's career. In the 1950's men got their hair cut every week and you'd wait for a long time at the barbershop on a Saturday morning. Then the Beatles happened, men let their hair grow and many good barbers had to look for another line of work. Time was when all businessmen wore a suit and tie to work and it was good to be in the business of manufacturing men suits. Then someone discovered the idea of business casual attire and business owners had to adapt.

Marketers and PR people try to anticipate the shifts in preferences and spot trends but it's very hard to do so before they manifest. The unfortunate reality is that most of the time trends are very difficult to see while they are building and only become evident to us when it's "too late" to take advantage of them.

In the late 1990's there was mass hysteria over the Internet stocks and IPO's. The general recollection people have about investing during that era is negative. People lost a lot of money. We forget that before all the losses came astronomical gains. Lots of people made fortunes. Many people hopped on the band wagon too late. The trend had run its course and was already poised for a very steep decline when most people made their investments.

As of the writing of this book, the stock market is at all-time highs, experiencing unprecedented growth in a ten-year bull-market run. Like anything that goes up, it must come down and when it does people will lose money and become jaded once again. "There's no way to make money in the markets," they will claim. The smart bet, however, is to understand and accept there is a decline coming and be positioned and prepared to take full advantage of it. Being aware of an outside influence can help you not only prepare for it, but take full advantage of it.

Keeping up with Social Media trends is the new "IPO". Facebook. Instagram. Twitter. Snapchat. YouTube. LinkedIn. Quora. And then there's Uber and Lyft. We live with change that is never ending and moving at breakneck speeds.

The Federal Government is a massive macro influence for Americans and ultimately the global economy. With rising gas prices and oil embargos, we might all be driving hybrid cars in 20 years and there's little anyone can do about it. And, that might be a bad thing if it happened. The economy is truly global. The internet has brought everyone closer together. The world is smaller than it's ever been. The economies in China, Japan, Russia and India do influence things, which influence other things, which influence other things, which influence you. Indirectly yes, but the influence is there nonetheless.

2. Segmented Micro Influences:
These are large influences that do not affect everyone but do factor-in for large segments of the population or groups of people. They include: the weather and

natural disasters (distinguished from normal weather patterns and fluctuations), the regional economy, industry trends in your business, the actions and decisions of the management of the company you work for, as well as competitors and suppliers.

In one of my past businesses we started off every year with a large sales training seminar and the launch of a new crop of Sales Reps, which gave every January a punch and started the new year off with a nice sales increase. It was a system I developed early on in my business career and I used it to become the top manager for the company I was working with at the time. We would actually run the seminar the week between Christmas and New Year's Day so they were ready to go on day one of the new calendar year. Back then I was working in Toronto, Canada where we were potentially impacted each year by the weather.

One year a severe ice storm hit the entire Northeast Corridor of North America the night before the seminar was supposed to begin. I mean, everything was covered in ice; the roads were not drivable and treacherous at best. People couldn't leave their houses. We ended up having less than 50% of the new sales reps that we should have had the storm not come or hit on a different day. So, the year started poorly. My entire organization was shell-shocked.

We had never had a January that wasn't better than the January of the previous year and they didn't know how to cope. We worked our way through it, of course, but the reverberations of that storm were felt for a couple of years and the directions of some careers were altered as a result of it. Think of how the weather affects the clothing business, the hardware business and the travel business just to name a few.

In the last quarter of 2007, the United States (and ultimately the world) business community specifically were rocked with the subprime mortgage crisis. I think we can say with certainty that many bright, hard-working, professional well-educated people worked for the financial institutions involved in the mortgage meltdown. They came to work each day, did their job well and had a career that was definitely on the right trajectory. But others were making fatal decisions, which damaged the course of their lives forever.

New disruptive technologies can emerge from a competitor. It's easy to see how Uber and Lyft have disrupted the taxi business. It's easy to see how Google and Facebook online ads have disrupted traditional newspaper advertising. It's easy to see how digital cameras disrupted the film camera industry. It's easy to see how Amazon.com has disrupted the retail industry. A supplier can get in trouble, causing a cascading set of problems for you and your company. A key employee can have a personal problem or family emergency or illness.

3. Personal Influences

Some outside influences are personal and affect only us. What particular set of teachers and coaches we have as we get our formal education (and what's going on in their lives that particular year) can make a difference. What happens in the careers of our parents or other decisions they make such as moving to a new neighborhood (or perhaps a new state) or getting a divorce or adopting children can be factors. Decisions made by people who will become influential in our lives before we even meet them are a factor. Maybe our favorite teachers had other options and could have just as easily ended up teaching at a different school. What if a decision by someone else would have resulted in our not meeting our spouse or the love of our life?

Several years ago I opened a wholesale-to-the-public furniture store in San Diego, CA. I learned the business quickly and within six months had doubled the space for inventory. As the business grew, I knew I was going to need some to expand and possibly open additional locations. One afternoon, I was at the gym and ran into a former business associate, Paul, who was now living in the area. He had mentioned to me that he was in transition, looking for a new opportunity so I asked him if he wanted to do some part-time work for me. To make a long story short, he came to work with me, I eventually sold the business to him and to this day he still runs the company many years later. It's the only full-time business he's ever owned. What if either one of us had not been at the gym that afternoon?

We've all heard the phrase "being in the (right or wrong) place at the (right or wrong) time." This is a simplistic way of acknowledging the effects of outside influences. Most crimes are random acts of violence and everyday dramatically affect a few (and sometimes many) people. There are surely things you can do to minimize your potential for being a victim, but sometimes it's unavoidable.

Every year many people are slain because they happened to be at a bank, or convenience store, movie theater, concert or jewelry store when it was hit. A few minutes one way or another would have made all the difference to them.

4. Inconsequential Influences

Every day, lots of things influence your life but life goes on without much difference one way or the other. We power ourselves forward and most of these inconsequential influences bounce off the armor we've acquired growing up. No two days are ever exactly alike. No two meetings are ever the same (unless your boss is a total bore). Yet, by the end of the day, we're often struck by the "sameness" of it all.

As I mentioned earlier, it's easy to observe these influences when you're driving a car. You want to get from point A to point B in the least amount of time (unless you're just out for a "ride"—remember those?) with the least amount of hassle and expense. If you've ever been on the road at 5:00 AM, well you've got the road to yourself and your trip is not affected very much at all by other people. You glide along; going where you want to go and (especially if the Highway Patrol isn't around) you can usually make pretty good time. Now, at 5:00PM in most cities it's a very different story. Your travel is hampered by thousands of other drivers. Usually, hopefully, their influence is inconsequential but you can learn a lot by watching for it. How often is there just enough room for a truck to pull out in front of you and let you enjoy the smell of diesel fumes or cause you to get stuck at a red light? Something delayed you just long enough to let the truck pull out. Maybe you made a green light earlier in the trip? Maybe you forgot something and had to go back into the house? Each and every ride we take is usually influenced by many such factors without giving them much thought. And so it is with life. Phone calls that we get, impromptu meetings, chance encounters all add up, along with the planned events, to make our day.

As you learn to watch for these inconsequential influences something else will occur to you. You will see their effects on many aspects of your life and their potential to migrate from not mattering to mattering very much. And as you become aware of them, you can use them to your advantage.

5. Incomprehensible Influences

The world we live in is a huge knotty place. To call it multifaceted is a gross understatement. Most of the factors that affect us we are aware of and acknowledge. But there are some that are beyond our comprehension or awareness. Our world, where we feel safe and (for the most part) in control, has some things going on beneath the surface. Sometimes they manifest themselves after the fact so at least we understand retroactively, but other times we're never exactly sure what was at work.

Acumen is vital to success in any field and people who have risen to positions of authority possess a great deal of knowledge about the inner workings of their organization. But, if you work in a large organization, regardless of your position, I can say categorically that you do not know everything that is going on around you. Furthermore, there are unseen dynamics in other companies you may rely on. Things happen all of the time that we cannot explain, even retroactively. We've all been party to many conversations like this: "What happened here?" or "How could this occur?" Answer: "Well, we're not exactly sure."

Nobody fully understands what drives the stock market, for instance; if they did, they would be rich beyond imagination, but the stock market is not "understandable." It is a complicated dynamic system, like the economy at large and therefore subject to forces beyond our comprehension.

Retired Fed Chairman Alan Greenspan is one of the wisest and most respected economists on the planet. He consistently demonstrated a grasp of the economy, which served the United States well throughout his tenure. I watched with interest his testimony to a senate subcommittee on the economy in late February 2002. Mr. Greenspan was asked if the economy would not have slipped into a recession in the fall of 2001 had it not been for the terrorists' attack of September 11th. Mr. Greenspan shot back without a moment's hesitation that it would be impossible to speculate how the economy "would have" performed. What struck me was that here we had arguably the most well-informed, brightest, most astute man there is on the subject, asked to look backwards and factor out the effects of a catastrophe event (as opposed to making a prediction) and his immediate response was essentially to say that it was impossible to do so. What does that tell us about anybody's ability to predict where the economy is going? It's just too complex. In fact, the word complex is terribly inadequate for describing it. It's more like "complex to the one millionth power." It's just too big to comprehend. All we can do is watch it unfold before us and try to understand what's happening and even that is a challenge.

Other influences we do not comprehend because we are not aware of them. We do not see allergens in the air or microbes in our food. We may become aware of them later when the symptoms of their havoc emerge. There could be something slowly going wrong in our automobile, our cell phone, our air-conditioner, or our body. Just because we don't see and aren't aware of these things doesn't mean they aren't there.

Within the atmosphere of these swirling influences, we navigate much as a skilled sailor does, using the wind and currents (outside influences) to reach his or her destination. Our life is a mosaic of experiences, encounters, interactions and ideas. Through our senses we each absorb a different set of factors, which again (over and above genetics) makes us unique because our lives are so different. The myriad of options and countless circumstances dynamically evolve and we reflect back to the world all that we see, hear, touch, taste, feel and think. The interplay between inside and outside influences produces this elegant choreography we call life. Its layers unfold and reveal its inner beauty much as a rose opening to the sun on a spring morning. This complex interaction is not something to be feared, but embraced, acknowledged and understood.

Influences in Context

Outside Influences come at us from many different directions and sources. Most people represent outside influences to us, and we to them. That is not to ignore our ability to influence others, which is very real and a valuable skill. But beyond that, as far reaching as it may be, other people can influence us in ways we cannot predict or react to.

At some level, and usually without note or consequence, outside influences affect us each day. Occasionally, they can have a significant impact (positive or negative). The more aware you become of their presence, the more you will see their effects. The better you understand them, as life plays out, the more opportunities you'll see to engage outside influences to your benefit.

We are all interconnected and the domino effect is a very real thing. It's also important to keep in mind that outside influences are a natural and ongoing part of a harmonious eternal system. The fact that we are beginning to realize their effects doesn't mean that they're just emerging now. Nothing could be farther from the truth. The pages of history (and events of prehistory) were co-authored by courageous, innovative, determined, motivated, passionate, hard-working human beings and outside, random events and influences.

 Catalytic Concepts

- Factors and forces beyond our control influence the experiences, direction, and outcome of our lives.
- A mokita is a truth we all know but agree not to talk about.
- Our mokita has been to not openly discuss or acknowledge these influences despite the irrefutable evidence of their existence.
- We swim through life in a sea of outside influences, many of which have no consequences but serve to signal to us the nature of our world.
- Outside influences come as random events and as the actions and decisions of others.
- They are varied in their scope with some that affect the entire planet, our country, our region, our company, our family and some just ourselves.
- We are all interconnected and we operate in the midst of a confluence of our own initiative and other dynamics.

CHAPTER 6
Future Block

"I never think of the future, it comes soon enough."
–Albert Einstein

Seeing the Future

H. L. Mencken said, "We are here and it is now. Further than that all human knowledge is moonshine." The desire to know and perhaps shape the future runs deep in all people but it can lead to frustration. Business people and investors strain to foresee the direction of the economy. In our lives, we all wonder about the future and what it may hold and we do our very best to influence it, occasionally with some degree of success.

We so want to know the future that a cottage industry is associated with trying to predict it. The "Psychic Hotline" draws tens of thousands of callers every week. It's not just lonely, lovesick people who want to know the future.

Corporations pay huge fees to trend-spotters and futurists. Some of them are quite good but predicting the future is a very difficult way to make a living.

One formula used by a company that supplies "hot tips" to people who bet on football games is actually pretty ingenious. They sent out hundreds of thousands of emails with a special free "pick of the week," except that half of the emails pick one team and the other half pick the other team. Obviously, half of them predicted the correct winning team. The company tracks who gets which mailer and they follow-up with the people who got the winning prediction with a new "pick of the week" for next week. But this time the information isn't free. Again, half are right, and so on, and they establish a record of success. Well, after a few weeks, the people who are "still in the game" are convinced this company has the system down. They tell their friends about it and they spend a lot of money themselves along the way.

People who deal in information about the future realize that if you make enough predictions, some of them are bound to come true. You can highlight and build on those successes and really convince people you know what's happening, and more importantly, what is going to happen in the future. Few, if any, such people or organizations have much staying power because eventually the massive pile of missed predictions catches up with them. The truth of the matter is the best that we can do is carefully analyze what is happening and what has happened and make some educated guesses by the future. Then keep our fingers crossed.

In today's day and age, this is no more apparent than in the Cryptocurrency market where experts and novices alike try to predict the rise and fall of Bitcoin. Now, I'm not going to try to explain what Bitcoin is nor am I going to suggest whether to invest or not invest in this new-age digital currency. However, as I'm editing this book, I just increased my holdings in several cryptos by more than 10%. For no apparent reason, other than outside influences, the market has suddenly dropped by $20 billion in less than 30 minutes. Of course, what goes down… and in the ever-changing world of Cryptocurrency, money is to be made as markets enter panic mode.

I'm not suggesting a new way to predict the future; there are enough of them out there already. I do want to address the practice of doing so and the risk associated with it. Remember the 1956 Oscar-winning best original song recorded by Doris Day, Que Sera, Sera (Whatever will be, will be)? It's all right to plan and predict as long as you keep things in perspective.

If you're a well-established business with a clear and stable history, you can usually hit the mark fairly well. The plan for this year is basically the same as the plan for last year, except bigger. Companies in the franchise business develop a highly refined model that just pops out locations and makes every effort to achieve a high degree of uniformity. I'm sure they're always looking for incremental improvements but the pattern of success is well established and to some degree it makes sense not to tamper with it. A business system can evolve, as sharks have, to streamlined perfection and they'll continue to replicate for a long time until something (often from the outside) disrupts them.

When you move out of the well-known into the un-known, things get a little sticky. I'm speaking here about those areas of life and business where innovation is required or at least desired. When you are reaching out into unchartered territory you just don't have as much to go on.

Predicting Audience Reaction

Television is expected to be in touch with the mood of the people watching it and must keep re-inventing itself. A cursory review of the television network's fall programming is simple evidence of how hard it is to predict how the chemistry will work on a TV show. There's no question that people in the top programming jobs of the major networks are bright, intelligent, hard-working people. They know their business like no one else. Yet, every fall, we're treated to programs that are absurd in their proposition, poorly written, poorly cast, and obviously ill fated. This doesn't mean that the people who make these decisions are stupid. It does mean that it's very, very difficult to get a television program right. It's a very involved mix of positioning, characters, writing, acting, directing and innumerable "intangibles." Most of the time they stay with the trends of that particular moment, the latest reality show, or what is hot at the time. Still, the vast majority of new shows fail.

Law and Order SVU has been on for 15+ seasons. And, even though the character development that takes place has withstood the test of time, the show continues to reinvent itself, change up the cast and do what is necessary to remain current.

Jerry Seinfeld's show is one of the most outstanding examples of a successful show from any era. Today, you can find a rerun of Seinfeld on TV or get your Seinfeld fix "on-demand" on any Netflix, Apple or Amazon device. Interestingly, with the exception of Julia Louis-Dreyfus, several of the main characters have attempted to parlay their unprecedented success on Seinfeld into success on a new television program only to be dashed against the rocks and end up in the heap of pulled television shows.

You can be sure that at some point in time, even the most ridiculous TV program idea made sense to a lot of really bright people. It's very expensive to produce a television program and it doesn't happen in a whimsical way. But the tastes of the viewing audience are, in fact, very difficult to assess and even the best television producers would be hard-pressed to recite a formula that would guarantee success.

Did you know that NBC, CBS and ABC all turned down American Idol? In fact, so did the executives at Fox. It was Rupert Murdock's daughter that convinced her father (who owned Fox network) to buy the show and of course it was a phenomenal success for 13+ seasons.

And then there are scenarios where a TV show is an instant hit. Take the latest release of the Rosanne show. Millions watched, making it the number 1 show on television. Then, Rosanne sent out an offensive tweet (perhaps outside influences impacting the writers, directions, producers, actors and fans of the show) and within minutes the show was cancelled. Outside influences can have both positive and negative effects.

The fact is that in almost any other kind of business, new programs (and here I mean marketing programs, internet programs or advertising programs, training programs, real estate programs, sales programs, affiliate programs or new products or services) are conceived, endorsed, supported, resourced and launched only to have them fall flat on their face, even within successful businesses.

There's always a lot going on below the water line. Very real influences beyond the perception (and certainly beyond the control) of the principles in any given human endeavor, a TV show or anything else, will have an effect. Sometimes those hidden influences cause a business, a project, or a person to stumble. Other times, for no explicable or understandable reason, they yield success. Oftentimes results fall somewhere in the middle. Rarely, but to the greater glory of those involved, they produce extraordinary results.

It's pretty much impossible to predict the future with any degree of accuracy. In Beautiful Boy (Darling Boy), a song John Lennon wrote for Sean, his second son, there is a wonderful line about life not always conforming to our plans. Ironically, the song was released in 1980 and on December 8th of that same year, John Lennon was tragically shot and killed at the age of forty by Mark David Chapman.

We like to think we're making our way through life, but at the same time, life kind of happens to us and we ride along with fascination. It's largely a "learn as you go" deal, and unfortunately, we don't get to practice; there's no dress rehearsal. You just suit up, and get out there and perform… it's show time!

Random Events Theory

A multitude of random events are constantly influencing our lives. Some outside influences are a result of the actions and / or decisions of others or are "systemic" in nature (affected by the economy, for instance). Other forces and factors are simply random, with no particular person or system as the root cause.

Early in my business career I developed something I called "Random Events Theory." In fact, this book is an outgrowth of that theory and thinking. What I saw all around me was evidence of the fact that some completely random factors, totally outside anyone's control, and in some cases even outside our awareness, often had a dramatic effect on the outcome of life and business situations.

Random events happen every day in our lives. Fortunately, the consequences are seldom dire. These events swirl around us and we hardly notice. Ever catch your belt loop on a door handle? How about when a phone charging cable gets caught as you are pulling it out of your purse of briefcase, just tangled enough to get stuck? Couldn't do that again if you tried. But quite often, as you go through your normal daily routine something unlikely (in the sense that the odds against it occurring are huge) happens.

Random Thoughts

Randomness occurs at the intersection of time, capability and options. One example we see every day, and I encourage you to give this careful consideration, is when we speak with others. That's a two-part equation, but let's look at your side first. Unless you are working from a prewritten (and pre-considered) script, for even the most eloquent and careful among us, speaking is a random event. I mean, we can have a pretty good idea of what we want to convey, and our vocabulary and communications skills enter into the equation, but a lot of times it's potluck in terms of the words that actually come out as we make our point.

Your mind makes hundreds of split-second decisions and the words come out, occasionally surprising even you. Have you ever been speaking and observed to yourself, "Hey, that sounded pretty good"? (I seem to make that comment a lot). What's interesting about this is that if you attempt later to recapture a particular phraseology, sometimes you can't do it—and you're the one who said it in the first place! I wonder, have you ever said something you were sorry for? I don't mean in malice or anger, just sometimes stuff comes out, or comes out in a way, that you wish you could do over. "Let me say that another way." (I seem to do that a lot as well.) I assume you'll agree with me on this, there is virtually nothing that you have more control over in your life that what comes out of your mouth. Yet, we oftentimes surprise ourselves with the sequence of words we string together. Now in a dialogue, that's "times two" (or more) because one person is reacting to the (somewhat randomly selected) words of another and responds in kind. It's no wonder that people have so much trouble understanding one another sometimes.

It is this random selection of words and formation of ideas that leads to the practice of "thinking out loud" for an individual, or "brainstorming" for a group. In fact, when I'm looking at future growth opportunities with my team, Scott might say, "I'm just brainstorming here…" and then continue with his thought. Sometimes improvisation leads to genius, which is almost always circumstantial and often relies on randomness as its source.

Written words can also demonstrate randomness and outside influences. Writing offers the benefit of lasting evidence, so the differences in the results of our thinking can be more stark and undeniable. Just sit down and write a couple of paragraphs on just about any subject (make it something enduring like the importance of family) and file that paper away. After a short while, without making any effort to reproduce the same answer (this is a test of creativity, not memory) start over with a couple of paragraphs on the same subject. You'll be amazed at how differently you'll go about it. The main point probably won't change, but how you say it will and in communicating, the words we choose to make our point matters a lot. You can repeat the exercise over and over and you will choose different words each time. I find that happens in the editing of this point. I'll work on a paragraph or a section and when I come back to it a few hours later it needs further clarification or editing.

Now, sure, you'll be in a different mood each time and other factors will have changed (which is the related point anyway), but the biggest factor affecting it is that the process is random. There are countless ways of making a point or describing a scene or concept. And, there are innumerable other little places in life where such events and processes are affected by randomness in much the same way.

Random Events Can Be Massive

Randomness is easy to spot around huge dramatic events in society. Shortly after the terrorists' attack of September 11, 2001, stories began to emerge of people who were in the World Trade Towers for the first and only time just that one particular day. At least one of the victims had taken several months to get a job with a company located there. She went all the way through the interview process. She waited patiently to find out if she'd gotten the job and rejoiced when she was informed she was hired. She was told to report for her first day of work on September 11th. There were also stories of others who worked there every day, for 25 years, but who were out sick or who had to travel that day and so they were not in the buildings when the plane hit. In the case of a tragic disaster, normally inconsequential decisions like calling in sick for a day can be life altering.

Consider the plight of the *Ehime Maru*, a Japanese fishing trawler on a training cruise off the coast of Hawaii in the Pacific Ocean. That's the largest ocean in the world, covering some 70 million square miles, one third of the earth's surface. Yet, on February 9, 2001, The *USS Greenville*, a nuclear-powered submarine, surfaced at speed and collided with and sunk the *Ehime Maru*. Nine lives were lost. What are the chances that those two ships would be attempting to occupy exactly that same spot in the ocean at that particular moment? And furthermore, that the collision would happen in exactly that way? The odds against it are astronomical, but tragically it did happen.

Another dramatic event with the United States and Japan as the principle players happened at the end of WWII. The U.S. dropped the second atomic bomb on the Japanese city of Nagasaki on August 9, 1945. (The first one, of course, was dropped on Hiroshima several days earlier.) Few people realize that Nagasaki was a secondary target that day. The primary target was the city of Kokura, approximately 175 miles away. When the bomber carrying the second bomb arrived over Kokura a thick blanket of clouds covered the city. The bombardier could not see through the clouds to set his sights on the target. The plane made several ominous passes over Kokura but to no avail. The captain of the flight decided to head for the second target on the list, Nagasaki.

Despite some cloud cover there, they were able to drop their payload and hit Nagasaki, taking close to 100,000 lives. The rain of death and destruction changed the course of life for many hundreds of thousands more that were left behind to mourn and rebuild. Think of how many Japanese today are descendants of the inhabitants of Kokura, the city that was spared. The random influence of cloud cover changed the lives of millions of Japanese in the decades to follow, and many more were never, and will never be born.

If dramatic events that change the course of history are influenced by randomness, doesn't it follow that, on a much smaller scale and hopefully in a less damaging way, they affect our lives as well? Does ignoring the effects of randomness yield more control, or less control? Acknowledging its influence, and the influences of other outside factors on your business and in your life, actually gives you better control because it yields better understanding. Misconceptions about the environment or denial of significant factors in a situation are not good planning tools. Even if those factors are not in your control it does make good sense to ignore them. A more complete understanding has to lead to better decisions.

Once you acknowledge randomness, you'll see it showing up everywhere. You see it plays a big part in how the world works. You'll marvel at its beauty and predictability—predictability in the sense that it is omnipresent. You can't escape it. You might as well learn to appreciate it. People who share this awareness learn to point it out to one another, and, as you do, your appreciation for it will grow. If you and a colleague both read this book, you'll undoubtedly have moments when, in a meeting, somebody is asking "How can this be happening?" You'll look at each other and say, "Outside Influences!" or "Random Events!" The more you "stir" these ideas in the kettle of your mind, the more richly they'll blend to provide you with intellectual nourishment. If your colleagues have not read *Outside Influences* yet, encourage them to get a copy of the book and read it so you can discuss it with them.

A Quark's Journey

Later, I'm going to discuss with you "Chaos Theory" from quantum physics and its application to our everyday lives. But, let me share one point from that discussion now as it relates to random events. In the field of study called quantum mechanics, scientists have discovered very small atomic particles called "quarks". These particles move in seemingly random patterns at very high speeds, usually over a defined field. There is absolutely no way to predict the direction they will take but experts have been able to track and map the path they follow. Unlike snowflakes, which are all different, there is no perceptible difference in quarks, yet no two quarks follow the same path.

The fascinating aspect of this is that, when scientists track the random flight of a quark over a defined plane long enough, a pattern begins to emerge. Like a flower opening to the sun, even this highly "random" particle of matter reveals a "purpose" and a grand design. I believe the same is true in our lives. Randomness is part of the system we live in and, over time yields a pattern as well. Not that it's pre-determined, but it is systemic.

The "Life Formula" Concept

Each event in our lives could be expressed in a lengthy, complex algebraic calculation with hundreds, if not thousands of factors leading to the result.

Each day would be a seemingly endless series of those calculations. Each person's individual life would require an almost infinite number of such calculations to represent all of the forces and influences affecting it. And, as in any calculation, changing the factors will change the outcome, and remember, many of those factors are not in your control.

How complicated would it be to try to capture a person's life in an equation? First, you'd have to identify all of the variables. There would be tens of thousands of them. Then you'd have to look at the interaction of the variables and the resulting new factors. The bottom line is that the events of your life are probably much more complicated than any algebraic problem you have ever considered unless you happen to be a rocket scientist.

Remember the classic sci-fi thriller, *The Day the Earth Stood Still?* If you haven't seen it, watch it on Netflix. It's great. There's one scene where the hero of the film, a human looking alien (traveling among us incognito) from an advanced civilization in a far-away galaxy is trying to get an audience with one of earth's leading scientists. Needless to say, the scientist is very busy and the alien is at a loss for how to get to see him. He can't just say, "I'm the spaceman everybody is talking about." So, to get his attention, the alien lets himself into the scientist's study. There, a lengthy problem is scrolled across a blackboard, filling it from top to bottom. The equation includes hundreds of factors (like the ones in "A Beautiful Mind"). The alien looks at it quickly, smiles knowingly, and makes a couple of adjustments and writes his phone number on the board.

The scientist called the spaceman later that day. He had found the spaceman's calling card.

Have you ever thought about different your life might have been if on any one of many occasions you had made a different decision? Keep in mind that these decisions need not have seemed like large decisions at the time but their subsequent ramifications could have been huge. Science fiction writers deal with time paradox questions a lot. In any sort of time travel there is always the obligatory lecture about not changing anything in the past, as even the slightest change could alter the course of history. They call this the *Butterfly Effect*. The point is the interconnectedness of all people, situations and actions; some things happen as a result of factors outside our control and our life is the result of the exquisite interplay between the two.

People "run into" one another all the time, in the hallway at work, at the coffee shop or food market. You're "channel surfing" and catch a commercial for something that interests you. You take one way home instead of another only to find a huge traffic jam. You leave for the airport for an International flight only to realize, once you arrive at the airport, that you've left your passport at home. The list of "coincidences" goes on and on. As you'll see later in the book, the evidence is overwhelming.

Catalytic Concepts

- Our desire to know and influence the future is strong.
- Despite our best efforts, predicting the outcome of new experiences can be very difficult.
- The vast complexity of life creates random events which occur without cause, rationale, or reason.
- Many things that happen in our lives are the result of random interactions and connections; random events can play a huge role in forging the future.
- Randomness is at the core of how life unfolds.
- Our "Life Formula" would be an incredibly long equation with endless variables and factors. Adjusting a single factor could affect the product of the equation and the outcome of an event, or of our life itself.

CHAPTER 7
Evidence in Nature

"Come forth into the light of things, let nature be your teacher."
–William Wordsworth

The Law of Averages and Massive Effort

Mother nature "understands" the law of averages and that massive effort is often needed to overcome negative outside influences and achieve success. Nature overpowers the odds; that's how life continues. Forces against life are everywhere in the environment. The planet is hostile even at the very top of the food chain. In addition to predators, new life must overcome many challenges. By putting forth massive effort, the initial factor in the equation of life is large enough that even a failure rate of 99.9% still results in success (the continuation of a species).

Every spring female Ridley turtles make their way to a beach on the Pacific coast of Costa Rica. Over a period of five or six days hundreds of thousands of them crowd over one another to find a bare spot of sand to dig their nest and lay their eggs. At the peak time 5,000 female turtles per hour are emerging from the sea to lay their eggs. Forty million eggs are laid in just a few days.

Now, when not nesting these turtles are spread out across the oceans leading relatively solitary lives. By nesting together in this way, they increase their offspring's chances for survival because predators are the biggest obstacle to their reaching adulthood. If the turtles just nested on any beach all spread out, the number of baby turtles would be very small and quite a manageable meal for a few sea birds. But this event is so massive in its proportions that it overwhelms even the most voracious of predators.

Millions hatch and head for the sea. Most do not make it but some baby turtles survive the gauntlet of the thousands of birds that congregate for the event every year.

Think about the number of acorns that a mature oak tree yields every year. These are produced at great cost to the tree, which uses up substantial amounts of energy to create them. Yet, every year each oak tree produces thousands of acorns. This process is required for the success of the species and is so ingrained that even in residential area, where trees are surrounded by streets, sidewalks, driveways and lawns—in other words, no chance for their offspring to succeed—they still produce thousands of acorns every year until they die.

Consider what has to happen for an acorn to become a healthy, mature oak tree… it must fall and bounce of be kicked or carried beyond the canopy of the parent tree. It has no chance of survival if it doesn't move away at least a little. It must come to rest in fertile soil where it will get sunlight and water. It will complete with very aggressive weeds and other trees as well as other acorns. Why, it's a one in a million shot. And this process is carried out, with slight variations on the theme, in each of hundreds of different species of trees. And thankfully, most of our world is covered with countless examples of those beautiful plants we call trees.

Now if acorns were people, the ones who made it to become mature trees would be applauded. They would be interviewed and win awards. They might write books and have their own YouTube channel with millions of subscribers. The ones that ended in piles on the forest floor in the fall would be looked at as less worthy, not diligent… "unsuccessful". It could be argued that all acorns are pretty much the same. Could It be that we humans are much more similar than we tend to think?

You can decide for yourself the relative value of the successful versus unsuccessful acorns (and people for that matter), but for sure, nature "understands" this phenomenon after eons of evolution. That's why each successful plant and each successful animal has the potential to produce thousands, if not millions, of offspring. Nature knows that many attempts at success won't make it and just overpowers the chances of failure with millions of attempts. Massive effort overcomes obstacles and ensures the success of some members of the species.

It is for this reason that human beings who desire to achieve success continue to move forward, continue to look for fertile ground, continue to plan themselves within opportunities that give them greatest chance to achieve their goals.

One species in North America releases millions of young adults into the world each spring. They are human high school and college students launching their careers upon graduation. Fortunately, we don't have to be concerned with predators but our young must run the gauntlet of life and deal with whatever unfolds before them. Maybe there are more similarities than meet the eye.

Lightning Strikes Twice

A recent news item reported about a home in the Philadelphia area that had been hit by lightning twice within the period of just a few months. This was an ordinary house in the middle of a residential neighborhood. It didn't sit alone up on top of a hill or anything… didn't have a 40-foot chimney. After examining the house, officials determined that there wasn't anything about it structurally that made it more prone to being hit by lightning. It just happened.

At first blush, when you think about it, having your house get hit by lightning once is pretty rare. People use the expression "You have a better chance of getting hit by lightning than you…" to describe something that is highly unlikely. I don't know anyone who's ever had had his or her house hit by lightning event one time. Do you?

Yet here's this poor family that just got all the repairs finished from the first strike and wham, they're struck again. Lori Ginsberg, what did they do to anger Thor? That's what the ancients would have concluded. This family must have done something to deserve this punishment. Something must have caused this curse since it's so rare for a house to be struck in first place, and with so many houses in America (probably around 75 million), what are the odds that it would hit your home a second time? Infinitesimal! Perhaps one in ten million.

Well, if it's one in ten million, and there are 75 million houses in the United States, it's likely that seven or eight homes will be struck by lightning this calendar year! The odds are small of that happening, but the number of possible targets is so large, the extremely unlikely happens from time to time. It's in our nature to attribute "causes" to things, but we seldom consider the massive number of possibilities in so many aspects of our lives.

The Flaw of Averages

Dr. Sam Savage, senior research associate at Stanford University, has written extensively about the potential for inaccuracy in mathematical and statistic models. Even assumptions based on high probability can be rendered false by the occasional highly unlikely occurrence. Furthermore, statistics and averages don't always tell us what we want to know. For instance, if the high temperature in a city is only 25 in winter and soars to 125 in summer, the average daily high may be 75, but the actual temperature would often be very uncomfortable. That's the flaw of averages.

Natural Selection

Between 1831 and 1836 a young man by the name of Charles Darwin sailed around the world as a naturalist observing everything from geological formations to the vast plentitude and geographical divergence of life on earth. Taken together with other theories and doctrines of the time, this led him to the theory of evolution via natural selection. One of the key observations Darwin made, which has subsequently been validated by extensive research, is that within a species, members of any one generation exhibited variation. In other words, you don't have to look back over thousands of years to find variation in a species; you can see it any time you want to by careful examination. A degree of variety is always present. You can readily see this by observing human race—the variations are limitless. While I do not intend to debate the theory of evolution here and now, I do want to focus on the variations.

Biologist C. H. Waddington observed an important conclusion of Darwin's work that most people missed because they couldn't get past the man descending from ape's idea. Let's set that aside for now and consider this point:

"The basic feature of Darwinism is its reliance on chance rather than on a simple determinist type of causation. All events that lead to the production of new genotypes, such as mutation, recombination and fertilization are essentially random. It is the major service of Darwinism to have broken the hold on our minds or notions of simple causation."

In other words, these variations are nature's way of adopting and making improvements and they are random. It's that adaptation that relates to the theories of *Outside Influences*. You see, these variations are not engineered or targeted. They are not a response to the environment. They are never present and occur randomly.

Normally, when conditions are constant the variations do not confer any particular advantage to the individuals who possess them. Natural selection does not hold that species adapt and evolve variations that respond to changes in the environment because that would take too long. Rather, variations are always occurring, and as the environment changes, which it often does, some variants have a greater chance of survival than others. In other words, natural selection involves randomly occurring change (the variations) that happen to be better suited to the changes in the environment, which also occur randomly. If a given variation in a changed environment increases the chances of an individual's survival, then individuals possessing that trait will be more likely to survive—and reproduce. As a result, the variations most suited to the prevailing environmental conditions are the ones that are "selected" and passed on.

Over a large number of generations, the general form of the species will change so that the variant becomes the norm. Darwin coined the phrase "natural selection" to describe nature's way of identifying traits that are better suited to the environment, comparing it to what he called "artificial selection" as practiced by animal breeders, who mate animals that possess traits desired and selected by the breeders.

Natural Success

Within our lives and careers both "natural" and "artificial" selection is happening all the time. Occasionally, something random will lead to something good. In cooking we forget to add a "vital" ingredient only to find that the food still tastes great. In business, many a great product was found to serve a different purpose better than the one for which it was originally designed and indented. Viagra was created as a heart medication until participants in a usage study reported an unexpected side effect.

From time to time it's possible that we make well-thought-out improvements that really produce positive benefits. We carefully consider a course of action, a strategy, which we implement to achieve success. But the right strategy might not be correct, because it was the best researched. It could be right in the same way that a variation in a species turns out to be the right variation. That's why the key in decision-making is to make the decision. We may not have that great of an influence on the outcome anyway. To often people are scared of making a decision for fear that it is the wrong decision yet it is this decision that will ultimately determine a successful outcome.

Surely the systems and forces that apply to nature and manifest themselves in nature are also at work in our lives. We evolve as human beings as we live our lives. Some of that evolution is the result of our direct efforts to improve and grow. Some of it results from random combinations of people, places, and things we're exposed to as we make our way through life. As we grow we display variation. We call it individuality. In some cases, it results in our being better suited to the ever-changing environment, in some cases not. For a long time, it was not cool to be a nerd. Now some of the richest men in the world are the kings of the nerds. That may be natural selection at its best.

Could the dynamics of natural selection be at work in determining which individuals and organizations are best suited for the changing world of tomorrow? Or is it the artificial selection of our own analysis, planning, anticipation and efforts that writes the script for our future? The central message of *Outside*

Influences is that it's the complex and elegant interaction of both from which the future emerges. They work together, in unison.

 Catalytic Concepts

- Nature "understands" the odds against success are great and responds with massive effort.
- Extraordinarily unlikely things can happen when the number of attempts is astronomical.
- A vast number of factors (and possibilities) and the nature of life itself, provide for the potential of limitless variation.
- Variety leads to improvement as conditions change and random variations become advantageous.
- What we see in nature also applies to our lives and businesses. People and organizations grow and evolve. Variations occur in this process and they are sometimes better suited to the changing environment, resulting in success. Natural selection is as much a part of business success as our planning and initiative.

CHAPTER 8

Evidence in Life

"For life unfolds, at the roll of the die, that's truth told, for you and I"
–Walt Whitman

A "Chance" Meeting

I f you learn to look for it, you will see evidence of outside influences and random events everywhere in your life on a very regular basis. Here's a very fortunate experience I had several years ago. You may have a similar story to tell.

I was sitting in my office, it was on a hot, summer Monday in August. August 12th to be exact. I was having an informal meeting with Kathy, my office manager, planning the fall calendar and travel schedule.

As the discussion continued, we decided that the business needed two additional team members. The first, a high-level customer service position to engage with customers insuring they have the best experience when dealing with our company and the second, a social media expert to expand our footprint online. I also mentioned that it would be ideal to create a third position for someone who has a base knowledge of in-person sales, live events, on-site admin and would be interested in traveling every other weekend to Singapore, Kuala Lumpor Malaysia, London UK, Sydney Australia and more. You get the point. Leave Thursday, come home Monday. 17 hour flights with a 14 hour time zone change. It sounds glorious until the second weekend.

We agreed to fill the first and second position and spend considerable time interviewing the ideal candidate for the third job opening.

Later that afternoon Kathy called me to inform me of a candidate scheduled for an interview on Tuesday at 10:00am. "She is perfect for the customer service opening", Kathy said. "I have worked with her on a previous assignment and I think she would a great addition to the team."

That particular Tuesday would have been my Grandmother's 85th birthday. She and I were extremely close when I was growing up and her impact on my life was immeasurable. I wasn't planning on coming into the office Tuesday but with some reluctance I agreed.

On Tuesday morning, on her way to the office, Kathy called to make sure I was already in. I was. However, I had totally forgotten about the interview. I was in "gym attire", totally unprepared for the interview. In fact, I think I was wearing a green tank top that happened to match the green fabric on my desk chair. At 10:56, as I was standing in my office, I could see through a big glass window, through the lobby and into the parking lot, the most beautiful woman I had ever seen. She had long, brown hair, a great tan, a sexy body, and a sparkling smile. I took a deep breath.

I was in love. Instantly. From first site. I knew immediately I was in big trouble.

I wasn't looking to meet someone. I certainly wasn't looking for a life-partner, at least not that morning.

To make a long story short, the interview lasted five hours. She had incredible customer service experience and was perfect for the job until I asked the question: "Do you have a passport"? She said "No, but I can get one." Then I asked her if she liked to travel. She said yes. I asked her if she had ever attended a seminar. She said yes, and that she loved it.

By the end of the 5-hour interview she was hired, but not for the position she interviewed for. She had more talent in her little finger than most people do in her whole body—she could learn the business and do it with perfection. More importantly, I never wanted this woman to be anything but to be by my side. We left for Australia 10 days later.

That beautiful young lady is now my wife, Lori. Today we have, between the two of us, five incredible children and six phenomenal dogs. (No, that's not a typo). We smile and talk of being each others "soul-mate". She is my best friend. She is my everything. She motivates me, inspires me and brings out the best in me. It could be argued that we were "destined" to meet and fall in love. Destiny is such a sweet and romantic concept, and there's a part of me that knows, with certainty, that were meant for each other.

Another explanation is that it was simply chance that Kathy scheduled the interview that day. Lori had other plans that day, but Kathy let her know the importance of the interview on that day so she made it happen. Either one of us could have "zigged" instead of "zagged" and who knows the possible outcome? Our entire lives might well have been very, very different. Surely, we were predisposed to like and love each other. We accept that this series of random events certainly produced positive results in our lives. It seems pretty certain that our family and our business (team) owe a lot to Kathy for scheduling that interview.

Or maybe it was my grandmother's "outside influence"—we did meet on her birthday, you know, as random as that might be.

What needed to happen for Lori and I to meet on that day? What set of random events needed to occur for the two of us to meet when we did? It's all perfectly imperfect in a world that is so predictable and yet totally random.

A random decision can lead to a very important one. But this is where some people have trouble with the idea. They want to believe that something else was at work there. Could it really have been my Grandmother? They can't accept that such an important part of life is totally random. They want it all to have meaning. Heck, I want it to have meaning.

What most people fail to realize is that there is tremendous beauty in randomness. The world evolves and changes every millisecond. Today, in fact probably right at this moment, people are meeting who will become life-long lovers and friends. Children are being conceived. People all over the planet are making life-changing decisions right now, this very second.

I have made it a hobby to ask married couples how they met. It is fascinating. Many people met at school or on the job, sometimes through friends or in social situations. Sometimes an informal matchmaker gets them together or perhaps they "met" online. Most of the time, you can see some random elements involved in bringing them together. A minor decision to have a job interview on a particular day at a particular moment in time (like I had with Lori) can have vast significance in your life. Choosing your life partner may be the most important decision we make in our lives yet the initial meeting is often the result of serendipity.

If you know how your parents met, you may see this randomness in that meeting (and rejoice that it occurred). In fact, our very existence as an individual human being is highly influenced by this process.

There's a lot more to it than just one meeting. Our parents were the result of two such encounters (our four grandparents) and it's safe to assume that the same random influences were at work here. There were four such meetings between our eight great Grandparents and eight random events that brought together our sixteen great, great Grandparents. It's kind of mind-boggling to think about it, but approximately 150 years ago (six generations) 64 people (our great, great, great, great, Grandparents) met in 32 random encounters, probably in several different countries. In just those few generations, there were sixty-three independent meetings resulting in… you (and any siblings you may have). And that's not the most amazing part. Wait until we look at genetics.

Some people's mindset will not allow them to accept that they are the result of all these random events. If you choose to believe that there was something else at work there, so be it. Whatever was at work you can't deny that all of those meetings had to take place (as well as many more if you really want to look into it). Call it density, fate, or the hand of God. They are all lovely concepts. So, too, is it beautiful to see and understand this exquisite randomness. To me it's a wonderful thing. It manifests a complex system that yields the uniqueness of our individuality.

Random Results

The randomness of life and the potential impact of random events crystallized for me many years ago. I was late boarding an airplane, the last passenger to get on the plane for that specific flight, and as I walked to my exit row seat I noticed Lou Ferrigno (the Hulk, I Love You Man, King of Queens, and so much more) sitting in a middle seat between two huge guys. Lou himself is 6'5" and 268 pounds of solid muscle.

I put my bag in the overhead, walked back towards Lou, tapped him on the shoulder and said something to the effect of "How do you fit in that little" seat. I wasn't trying to be rude—we've already discussed how random words can be spoken out of turn. Then I turned around and went back to my seat.

That was it. I just met Lou Ferrigno, one of the greatest body builders in history and definitely a famous movie star. Perhaps I just insulted him—he did look angry—but at least I was now "friends" with the Hulk. Maybe not.

I didn't think about it much until a few days later. Four days to be exact. As I stood in line to board the plane, I felt someone punch me in the arm. Hard. It was Lou Ferrigno. He held up his ticket, pointed to it, and said to me, "first class.". Enough said. Then he walked on the plane. I must have made some impression on him for him to remember me four days later.

What Lou didn't know at the time was that I also had a first-class ticket. I boarded the plane and as I was sitting down in the seat I noticed that I was sitting next to, you guessed it, Lou Ferrigno. He looked at me with disdain. I'm glad he didn't turn green.

In that almost five-hour flight from Orlando to Los Angeles, Lou explained to me how he thought I had taken his seat on the initial flight to Orlando. We laughed and joked about it. At the end of the flight we exchanged numbers. It turns out that Lou lives just a couple of blocks from my house.

Since our first random meeting, and our even more random second meeting, Lou and I have become close friends and that created a long-lasting relationship that I truly value. But for a moment let's make a deeper analysis of what took place. Think of the randomness of meeting someone on a 3,000 mile flight and then four days later meeting on yet another flight.

Consider that he remembered me because of my insensitive comment on the first flight. Then, there is the randomness of sitting next to him on the second flight. We can be sure that many small decisions were made, for these situations had to happen such as choosing a flight to take, an airline to choose, and a seat to pick. In addition, the chance of this happening against is virtually impossible.

Who Wants to Be a Millionaire?

It takes a smart, quick-witted person to win this exciting game show. You can't be invited to try out unless you win a phone competition. Then you have to win at the try-outs. Then you have to win the "fastest finger" to get into the hot seat. Despite how the pressure makes some of them appear otherwise, just to get to play you've got to be pretty smart. And, for those who win it, you can rest assured that outside influences played a big part in their winning. You might say, wait a minute, they answered the questions correctly. They studied and knew the answers (or their "phone-a-friend" did). What's random about that? Let's look at it.

If you've ever watched the show, you know that the questions get progressively harder and harder as the dollar value goes up. The key is—what's a "hard" question? It's one you don't know the answer to. The low value questions are pretty much common knowledge (although on a rare occasion someone will get stumped by one of them). You can increase your chances of winning by study. The more facts you can cram into your head, the better your chances that you will know the answer to the question asked. However, no matter how much you study, what you know will represent only a small percentage of the total body of knowledge from which questions can be drawn. Conservatively, a really bright person would only know somewhere between five percent (most smart people) and ten percent (a virtual genius) of the answers but I'd guess the number is even smaller. So, for people who do win big money, when it looks like they win because they are really smart, it's actually much more because random events presented them with the questions that they happened to be able to answer. There are far and away many more questions that could just as easily have been asked that they would not have been able to answer.

The more you look into things, the more you'll see the effects of outside influences. They even affect mechanical systems, as I learned as at a recent school field trip with my 5th grade daughter.

The Bell Curve and School Field Trip

For my daughter's fifth grade school field trip, her class went to the Santa Monica Pier Amusement Park. This is always a highlight for kids and fortunately enough I was able to chaperone on the trip. On this day, as we entered the park, there was a special attraction that was very impressive.

The display consisted of two large pieces of clear Plexiglas about 5 feet high and 10 feet across. They were set about 3 inches apart (creating a form like a giant "Ant Farm"). Within and between the pieces of Plexiglas were hundreds of "pins" like you might see in a "pinball" game.

The display was sealed on the sides and top except for a small opening (about 2 inches) at the top center. In a line across the bottom of the display were about 40 clear plastic tubes, each around 4 feet long and 3 inches in diameter. One at a time, a machine dropped white ping-pong balls into the exact same spot at the top center of the display. One after another dozens of balls were dropped in continuous flow. The designers of the display went to great lengths to be certain that each ping-pong ball was released in precisely the same way. The ping-pong balls bounce and careen off the pins as gravity pulled them down into the tubes at the bottom of the display where they accumulate one on top of the other as they filled up the tubes. As the tubes filled at different rates, they created essentially a bar graph, with some collecting more balls than others, and a pattern began to emerge.

What do you think the graph showed? The best curve! Despite the fact that each ball was dropped in exactly the same way, they did not follow the same path. The "environment" was tightly controlled. Most of the balls did drop almost straight down, filling the tubes in the middle of the display. Some bounced around a little and ended up close to the center tubes but a little over to the left or to the right. And somehow, certain ping-pong balls, not many, made their way all the way to the extreme sides of the display, some to the far left and some to the right. This happened for no apparent reason and with no scientific explanation other than the fact that, within systems, there is always a divergent behavior.

Of course, there are many differences between our lives and the random bounces of ping-pong balls; many differences, but also some similarities.

Income Distribution

Income distribution in 2017 shows a traditional bell curve. In other words, in this endeavor (the system of compensating people for their efforts) some people do extremely well, some people do extremely poorly, and most end up clumped around the middle. Stop and think about it, what else could a graph of income distribution possibly look like? Now, there's nothing at all predetermined about where you end up on that curve, but the fact that most people are going to be somewhere around the average is irrefutable and will not change. So is the fact that some people will earn very low income and some people will earn extremely high income.

This is an example of the over-riding power of the system. Conceptually, we are able to see that outside influences can create circumstances for some people that become impossible to overcome and their opportunity for fortune fades. That happens enough times to enough people and becomes readily apparent in their behavior and attitude. Once you grasp that, it's not too much of a leap to realize that it all works in reverse direction on occasion as well.

The dynamic evolving system called the economy creates opportunities and catastrophes every day. Complicated interactions occur among all of the factors involved, resulting in commerce and business trends. The machination of all of these elements creates the circumstances that we navigate and those that, to a degree, carry us along with them. We actively and intelligently search for currents and try to manage the wind. When everything comes together just right, extraordinary things occur. Sometimes the odds are overwhelmingly stacked against us. Most times, a delicate balance emerges and we manage to keep centered between catastrophe and spectacular success.

The Domino Effect

So many things happen in life "as a result of" other events. Some of the time we just move along smoothly without much turbulence. Other times, factors we aren't even aware of set off a chain of events that influence us. If you're curious and start to pull on the lose strings of life, you'll be amazed at what you can unravel. I make it a habit to ask questions about why things happen in a certain way. It's enlightening to do so. You really can begin to see the workings of the system. An intricate pattern of dominos can all be knocked over by just the slightest tap on the right one.

Consider this real-life experience of my friend Barry. One morning, as he is taking his 5-year old daughter to school, she cries out that she forgot her Teddy Bear. Barry, frustrated but mindful of the consequences of not having the Teddy Bear at school, turns around and heads back to the house. He pulls into the driveway, parks the car, makes a mad dash into the house, grabs the Teddy Bear that was sitting on the floor near the front door, and is back in the car in less than 2 minutes. Quickly, he's back in the car and heads off to day care. As he is going into school with his daughter, he notices a familiar looking person coming out that had just dropped off his child. It turns out they went to high school together... haven't see each other in years. They exchange numbers and agree to have lunch the following week.

Over lunch they catch up with one another about family and career. Both gentlemen are very accomplished executives in their own right. It turns out the man that was leaving the day care is looking to fill a position in his company. And it just so happens that Barry is not only looking for work, but is perfect for the position. To this today he still holds a high level executive position in the company, all because his little girl forgot her Teddy Bear.

Catalytic Concepts

- Outside Influences and random events part of our everyday lives. They are interwoven with our own decisions, plans and actions to create the fabric of life.

- Thinking through the process of our parents meeting, and their parents meeting, back through several generations reveals the random core nature of life.
- The effects of random events are usually subtle or inconsequential, but occasionally they can be massive, or tragic.
- The bell curve applies to many events and endeavors and demonstrates the systemic nature of randomness and outside influences.
- The complexity of life does not yield a complete picture to us. To some degree we must recognize that we are functioning with limited knowledge and awareness.
- The domino effect is interwoven in many aspects of our lives. Events, actions and decisions can reverberate through many levels of relationships.

CHAPTER 9

Evidence in Sports

"You can never know at the start of a game that it won't be some quirky bounce of the ball that decides the whole season."
–John Madden

Sports Mimic Life

The classic struggle for success is captured in the beauty and drama of sport. Sports and athletics offer us a way to participate in or observe a pure competitive activity that doesn't involve nearly as much chance as life itself. That's part of the beauty and appeal of spectator sports; compared to life, they are simple, clean, and easy to understand. The game takes place within a tightly defined field, court, track, etc. The boundaries keep the participants in, but did you ever stop to think that they also serve to keep other factors and influences out, at least for indoor sports?

Despite the boundaries, outside influences and random events play a small role in sports as they do in life. As in determining our overall success, they occasionally influence the direction of a game, a season, or an athlete's career. As a reminder, by far the most important factors in the success of athletes (as is true in business, relationships and life as well) include the following: desire, work ethic, dedication, conditioning, and their skill and knowledge of the game. These "inside influences" matter most. Sports are popular because outside influences can be kept to a minimum. We can grasp the key elements involved and we don't get bushwhacked by unconsidered consequences of hidden agendas or unseen dangers. With the exception of the weather (for games played outdoors, the weather is outside of everyone's control, yet can play a significant role in the outcome of the game) we pretty much know what we're dealing with in sports.

Beyond the weather, randomness still enters into sports, but nowhere nearly as much as in life. When you have a sport with multiple team players, randomness is exponential because, to some degree, the decisions and actions of the players are random, particularly in a sport like basketball where players have almost total freedom as to where they can go on the court. There are some set plays (which rarely go exactly as they are drafted) but for the most part, players are moving intuitively, responding to the movements of their opponents and teammates. Thousands of split-second decisions are made sometimes resulting in a great play, sometimes in a miscue.

Not only do you have ten players making thousands of decisions and counter-decisions throughout the game, but also you have coaches and referees that enter the mix. Then of course, you have the ball that can from time to time do some amazing things. How many basketball games have been decided when the ball seems to defy the laws of gravity and hang on the rim or come up out of the basket? SCORE!… maybe not! Have you ever seen a ball bounce off of a player's head while going for a rebound and bounce into the hands of a player from the other team who takes it for a score? It's amazing when you think about it but, if you consider every game of basketball that has ever been played in the 100-year history of the sport, there have never been two that were exactly alike.

The same is true of football where you have eleven players on each team and the unusually shaped pigskin. The single most remembered play in the history of the National Football League decided a Championship and could well have changed the career of dozens of players. Known as the "Immaculate Reception" the play involved the Pittsburgh Steelers and the Oakland Raiders. With seconds remaining and the Steelers down by several points, quarterback Terry Bradshaw fired a pass to one of his wide receivers who was well covered. The ball bounced in a weird way, off of the two players, up 20 feet into the air… and right into the hands of Steeler fullback Franco Harris, who took it in for a touchdown as time expired, giving the Steelers the Championship.

In sports it's skill, athleticism, conditioning, practice, hard work… and random events. The "element of chance" causes some crazy things to happen. And because decisions must be made in fractions of a second, with very limited information to go on, even conscious decisions are random to a degree.

Pure Competition

The element of chance makes sports interesting. Random events affect "sports" much more than "athletics" and the distinction is pretty clear although the criterion (chance) has become obscure. It's a sport if the competitive event is called a "game" (football, basketball, hockey) and there's a significant element of chance involved. It's athletics if the competitive event is called a "meet" or a "match" (track and field, swimming, tennis, wrestling). Athletics is more of a pure competition with little or no randomness. You "play" a sport. You "participate" in athletics. A game (sports) has a winner and a loser (except in the case of a tie, and often-times the teams just keep playing and playing until there is a winner). In some athletic events, even the person who comes in third "wins" a bronze medal. The language reveals the underpinnings of the activity. As with any game that you play, chance enters into sport.

In fact, games do not always determine who is the better team. You just can't do that in one game. That's why the NBA and the NHL and Major League Baseball determine their championships through a series instead of a single game (well, that and the fact that revenue from a series is many times higher). A series minimizes the effects of chance. That's why, on "any given Sunday" in the

NFL, one team can beat another. Underdogs win quite often; just ask the New England Patriots, winners of Super Bowl XXXVI about that (they were 15 point underdogs).

Athletics offers perhaps the purest form of a physical activity but isn't completely devoid of outside influences. Obviously, conditions such as weather sometimes have to be contended with. Also, the caliber of the competition in any given year, in any given event is random. The gold medal performance this year might have been only good enough for third place last year, or next year. Needless to say, especially after the 2014 Winter Olympics, any event that involves a judge or judges is very susceptible to outside influences.

But for the most part it's about who performs in this specific event, on this specific day, in the fastest time? Who can jump the highest, or the farthest? Who can throw a weight the farthest? Faster. Higher. Farther. It's a relatively simple equation. That is part of the appeal and beauty of the Olympics, which also has all the pageantry, imagery and history of the worldwide stage. As a result, the Olympics are enthusiastically anticipated and gather a large global audience.

But athletics occur at many levels all year long. There's no comparison between the number of people who watch college football or basketball and the number who watch college track or swimming. Chance adds excitement. For some spectators, athletics are a little boring because the element of chance has been engineered out. Popular sports have a lot of chance and random factors. As soon as you add a ball to the mix, and other team members, the equation becomes much more complicated, especially if that ball happens to be a strange elongated shape like a football.

Picture Perfect

An HBO Sports Documentary, which aired on January 21, 2002, shed some particularly interesting light on the subject of randomness. *Picture Perfect*, produced by Joe Lavine, with Executive Producers Ross Greenberg (President, HBO Sports) and Rick Bernstein (Executive Producer, HBO Sports), explored the remarkable impact that still photography had in shaping the sports history of America. The fascinating part to me was that they also interviewed the photographers of famous sports photos and brought out the story of how they got the shot.

The storyline was pretty much the same in each case, but I was really mesmerized by the tale related by Neil Leifer, the photographer who took probably the most famous boxing photograph in history. In the photo, Neil caught then Cassius Clay (now Mohammed Ali) standing over and taunting a knocked down Sonny Liston. A young Clay, in fantastic shape, glaring down at the old bear after the first-round knockdown that ended their second fight.

Leifer's recollection was vivid and honest. As a rookie photographer, he was assigned to the fight for *Sports Illustrated* along with a veteran who was one of the leading sports photographers of the day, Herbie Shockman. As the senior member of this two-man team, the elder "pro" got his choice of where to set himself up. Herbie took a prime spot, front and center at ringside. He was actually able to rest his camera on the canvas of the ring floor. Neil, who actually got "the shot", was relegated to a seat off behind a neutral corner.

It was amazing to hear Leifer explain how it all came about. "I was simply given Row A, Seat 13, as I remember it. I was really in a terrible position but it made no difference to me. I was just there, kind of as a back-up. Herbie was right there at point blank range with nothing in his way. I was sure he'd get several shots as filler for *Sports Illustrated*—crowd reaction, stuff like that. As it happens, in the first round Clay catches Liston with a haymaker and down he goes. Now, I gotta tell ya, from where I was standing, if I would have been able to stage this shot—'Sonny, I want you to lay right here in this position and Cassius, I want you to stand over him right here and glare down at him and do something dramatic'—if I could have had total and complete directorial control, I couldn't have set it up any better. In a million years, it couldn't have happened in a better spot for me. There, right in front of me it all occurred in an instant. I was ready. I snapped and bam—there you have it, the most famous boxing photograph ever taken. And what was so ironic about it was, there, forlorn and frustrated, framed between Clay's legs in my picture, was Herbie, just watching and looking helpless, while I made history. In truth, I just think I got lucky. Look, I'm not being modest when I say this, but at least 50% of sports photography is luck, at least 50%. I mean, what are the odds?"

What are the odds, indeed? Sometimes an apparent disadvantage is turned into an advantage. Over the last 50 years, *Sports* Illustrated has had hundreds; perhaps thousands of photographers work for them. Few have ever risen to the heights that this photographer has and he acknowledged the influence of factors outside of his control, which created the moment of his genius. True, he had to be ready to take advantage of it and to his eternal credit, he was. But so many factors also came into play; it would be difficult to list them all.

Team Sports

Randomness can dramatically affect the career of an athlete at any level. Few if any get to pick their coaches or teammates. Coaches have a major impact on the team's success and each individual player's career. It's not at all uncommon for a highly recruited high school player to pick a college and coach to play for, only to have the coach leave (or be asked to leave) before the player graduates. And furthermore, in team sports, the other players on the team largely determine your ultimate success.

Even a truly great player can carry a team only so far. Look at the career of Lebron James. Lebron is widely considered one of the greatest basketball players of all time (he is still active in his NBA career) and his record-breaking stats prove that. Lebron has won multiple championships throughout the years. In fact, he led two different teams (Miami and Detroit) to the NBA finals for 7 consecutive years. As an intense leader who wanted to win every championship with every fiber of his being, his winning percentage is less than fifty percent. Some critics say that "Lebron can't win the big one." Are you kidding me? This guy is one of the best, if not THE best player to ever play the game since the inception of the NBA. Basketball is a team-oriented sport. No one player is capable of bringing a team all of the way. There are many NBA players who have Championship rings that couldn't hold a candle to Lebron. Outside influences determined that for him, and for them.

A Flash of Genius

Genius if often situational. An artist has an inspiration at that particular moment with that particular mixture of colors on his or her pallet, painting that particular subject on that particular day. Change any of those factors and you change the painting. There is little that we do that is not tied in many ways to other factors in the situation. Occasionally these factors affect things negatively, usually they're pretty neutral, and sometimes they help create genius.

Every once in a while, a group of people comes together, at just the right time, with just the right chemistry, and just the right circumstances... and something truly extraordinary happens. Being part of something special is one of the optimum human experiences we can have—humanity at its best... life at its best.

In the music industry, there's something called "a one-hit wonder." An artist or group creates one song that has all the elements of a smash hit and is well received by the public, but they can never put it together again, never duplicate that particular sound. This happens in all fields of endeavor including sports, sometimes with legendary results.

Consider the 1980 U.S. Olympic Men's Hockey Team and their gold medal performance. If you could ever recreate the semi-final game between the USA and the USSR (which of course, you couldn't), it is unlikely that the outcome would be the same. The Russian team was more experienced, more talented, and had played together much longer. But the emotion, energy, and pure desire of the U.S. team was formidable. That, coupled with the random events that play a role in any hockey game, combined to create a most memorable sporting event for America, and a dreadfully forgettable one for Russia.

Mark Zuckerberg, CEO of Facebook invited 5 people to his Harvard Dorm room 11 years ago to discuss a business opportunity. Only 2 people showed up and they got in. Today, those two people are billionaires; Dustin Moskovitz and Eduardo Saverin. I often wonder about the three people who chose not to attend, for whatever reason they deemed valid at the time.

Maybe you've been part of something truly special in your life—one of those optimum experiences where everything falls into place and all of the participants blend together, each amplifying the other. Clearly, that's genius and sometimes we forget that the spark of genius strikes more often than you might think.

Sports are a living metaphor for life because they combine the elements of talent, ability, preparation, and desire with outside influences and random events. We get to see the whole drama played out in an hour or so with a nice neat conclusion. Somebody wins and somebody loses. Life is far more complicated and hopefully a whole lot longer.

Through sporting activities, games give us clear evidence of one of life's really important lessons. Something we are explicitly and specifically trying to do can still involve randomness. One example, in an incredibly simple activity can be extrapolated to far more than involved and prolonged activities and still hold true. It's randomness that creates situational genius. It's the combination of many factors, brought together at a single moment in time, for a limited time (which could be a minute, a day, a year, or a decade) that creates a unique opportunity for people to transcend normal limitations and achieve something spectacular.

Catalytic Concepts

- Combining the elements of talent, ability, preparation, and desire with outside influences and random events, sports mimic life.
- Applying the metaphor of sports to business and life shows the importance of commitment and hard work, but also the influence of good fortune.
- The element of chance makes things fun.
- It is possible to specifically be trying to do something, to concentrate your best efforts in the attempt, to have it happen just as you planned (the 60-foot putt), yet acknowledge that it was lucky that it occurred.
- There are many facets of sports and life, such as the caliber of our teammates and/or our competition at a given point that can influence success.
- Randomness creates the circumstances of situational genius.

CHAPTER 10
Evidence in Science

"Ethical axioms are found and tested not very differently from the axioms of science. Truth is what stands the test of experience."
–Albert Einstein

The Miracle of You

My mom had a twin sister. My wife has twins (a boy and a girl). In both cases, neither set of twins are identical, they are fraternal, meaning they don't look alike. There is certainly a strong family resemblance and they all acted very much alike (in their own unique way). Yet, of course, each is a unique individual.

This got me wondering about human variation. In other words, setting aside the obvious physical limitations, how many different human beings could one male and one female conceive.

I did some research and contacted experts in the field of genetics—a science that has brought new insights into the concept of human life and the miracle of you. The results (which I will summarize for you) are fascinating and help to make the argument that randomness plays a great part in our lives. You'll see it at the root of the answer to the very question of who you are.

Chromosomes are the genetic plans for a human being. Genes are arranged in a linear fashion along chain-like DNA molecules, which are coiled within chromosomes. They dictate the development of the fetus and provide the blueprint for our appearance, our intelligence, and a major part of our personality and health. We have two sets and there are 23 chromosomes each. We have one set contributed by our father and set contributed by our mother. The combination of chromosomes that occurs at conception is what determines, to a very large degree, the person we are. Each child born is the specific result of that set of chromosomes uniting.

The number of possible combinations of chromosomes between any couple is something on the order of 10 to the 15th power.

However, the actual number is even higher due to the "switching" of genes during meiosis. During meiosis, which is when the egg and sperm are dividing and separating their pairs of chromosomes into sets, genes are sometimes swapped across the chromosomes. Obviously, this swapping dramatically increases the number of possibilities because whole new genes emerge as a result of the switching. We do not know how often this occurs but considering the impact conservatively, the number of possible combinations is probably more like 10 to the 20th power (and potentially even higher). That's a 1 with 20 zeros behind it so the odds that you would be born, exactly the way you are, amount to:

100,000,000,000,000,000,000 to 1

Yes, you are indeed a miracle. The randomness isn't a coincidence—it's systemic. It's built into the wonderful system of reproduction. In fact, it's likely that the combination of chromosomes that each of us represents is unique in the entire history of mankind (that's why DNA testing is so accurate). Keep that in mind the next time you meet someone. Remind yourself how unique they really are and how they are a manifestation of this beautiful process.

Some people will want to believe some sort of divine intervention occurs at the moment of conception and that's fine. They may be the same people who argue against evolution by saying, "I am not descendent from a monkey!" There are several scientific arguments against evolution but the idea that a link between humans and apes is somehow degrading to us is not one of them. (Rumor has it that there's a similar simian denial circulating in the ape world, "Don't blame US for humans!"). Those same people who claim they could not be related to the apes will say they could not be the result of some random combination of chromosomes. Okay, fine. But what is for sure is that we as parents cannot pick and choose the characteristics of our children. That power sits outside of us, at least for now.

Earlier in this book we looked at the randomness of different people meeting, falling in love, and having children. Obviously, if our father and mother had not met, we would not be here. We now see that the same parents, our parents, could well have conceived a different person. In other words, just because our parents met and had children, does not mean that we had to be born. At each and every procreative act, a healthy human male releases 200 million sperm. Each one of them is carrying with it the possibility of a different person. For whatever set of reasons, the sperm that represented YOU succeeded at the moment of conception.

As I discussed with you earlier, I believe in the system that was set in motion eons ago. Within that system, there is a controlled randomness that results in the tremendous diversity of human talent, appearance, personality and character. We are a species rich in differences and I think that helps to make life interesting.

Incompleteness Theorem
It's not common to think this way, but a business is essentially a "system" (or system of systems). The successful business is a system that makes money. I choose to describe it that way here to help emphasize its complexity. Once you understand that a business is a system, you can look outside of normal business theories to gain further insights into how businesses work by looking at how other systems work.

The more you examine just about any system, even the relatively simple ones, the more you begin to see aspects of them that are very difficult to explain or understand. In 1931 the Czech-born mathematician Kurt Godel, developed something he called "Incompleteness Theorem," which provided that logical systems contained questions that can't be fully or accurately answered. He demonstrated that within any given branch of mathematics there will always be some propositions that couldn't be proven either true or false, using the rules and axioms of the mathematical branch itself. I think there are implications from this for life in general and all logical systems.

If you've had any number of years of experience in business, I can state categorically without knowing you and without knowing what business you're in, that you bump into things on a pretty consistent basis that you cannot understand. Certainly, virtually every business that I've been part of for the last thirty years has had these "unexplainable phenomena." Sometimes they can have a very positive effect. I can definitely remember looking at sales numbers and shaking my head wondering what was driving those fantastic results. Other times, a lack of results defied all logic and analysis.

I want to emphasize that accepting the incompleteness theorem as it applies to your business does not mean passively accepting aspects of it that you do not understand. Successful professionals will always work diligently to find the answers to key questions. Applying the incompleteness theorem to your business will help you maintain your sanity. Nothing is more frustrating than analyzing a problem and seeing a portion of your business behave in a way that makes absolutely no sense. At least now you will understand that because your business is an intricate complicated system, some aspects of it will be beyond your ability to fully analyze and comprehend.

Taking the entire analysis one step further, this applies more generally and more broadly to life itself. We've all witnessed circumstances and events in life that don't follow a logical pattern—that don't seem to make any sense. These things can cause severe frustration and anguish. That's a very understandable human reaction and should be less intense for you now because you'll see these inexplicable factors as outside the scope of information that is apparent or in any way available to you at that time. It's life's way to playing hide and seek.

Chaos Theory

I first learned of Chaos Theory (also known as complexity theory—which I think is a far better but less recognized name for it) some ten to fifteen years ago. The idea of chaos is married to complexity (thus the dual names) and refers to what might be called ordered disorder. Applied mathematics has been mostly concerned with the solutions of linear differential equations. Recently attention has shifted to non-linear differential equations, which predicted that small changes in the original conditions could sometimes make vast differences in complicated systems. The idea is that everything is interconnected though not in readily identifiable ways. The famous example is that of a butterfly fluttering its wings and causing a hurricane on the other side of the globe.

Through their analysis of chaos, scientists have discovered similar patterns underlying many separate and diverse fields. The discovery of fractals (and other new distinctions in quantum physics) helped explain that a graph showing the fluctuation of cotton prices is remarkably similar to one showing the changing population of a species of algae living in a pond. Obviously, these two phenomena have absolutely nothing to do with one another, yet thorough analysis clearly indicates a corollary relationship. How can this be? Chaos Theory demonstrates that there are underlying principles that affect all complex systems. The application of Chaos Theory is starting to spread from physics, mathematics and biology to organizational and other "human" sciences. It now facilitates the cutting edge of study in artificial intelligence, economic theory, and even political models.

It is becoming widely understood that within all complicated systems there are underlying pattern and predictability that guide the systems' dynamic nature. Our society is a complex system. Our economy is a complex system. Your life, your business and your career are subsets within these systems. We all operate on the "edge of chaos" balanced between an ordered, well planned, stable environment and a chaotic, unpredictable, intuitively understood world. The forces, which influence that world, are in some cases subtle and imperceptible. It other cases they are tectonic in their proportions and dramatic in their effects. There are patterns that dictate the evolution of the system.

We may not be able to predict the influence of chaos on our lives but it's foolish to ignore it. Pretending it's not there will not make it go away. The ostrich still has to contend with the problems confronting him even though he sticks his head in the ground. Even a simple kaleidoscope like we had as kids never presents exactly the same pattern to us twice. Neither does life itself. As we rotate a kaleidoscope, the objects inside tumble and fall and rearrange themselves; each new twist representing different positional relationships. Each new set of relationships creates a beautiful new pattern. Though very simple, this models our life in its ongoing evolution and stages. With each new twist and turn along the path of life, new and different opportunities and possibilities emerge. The adventure of life is truly fascinating to behold in its order and chaos.

I recently discussed the ideas of Outside Influences with a dear friend. A bright, well-read man, he is also highly accomplished and a firm believer in the traditional cause and effect approach to success. It was a lively discussion to be sure and after about an hour of dialogue, in response to one vivid example I shared with him of a random event which created a tremendous opportunity for a person we both know, still debating he said, "Well, if you look at it like that, everything is random." I waited a couple of seconds and simply replied, "I rest my case."

Universal Proportions

The size and scope of the universe is mind-boggling. The question of life on other planets fascinates us and justifiably so. Could there be intelligent life elsewhere? Of course, the answer to that question is, "Yes there *could* be." "*Is* there life on other planets" is a different question. When you consider that there are hundreds of billions of stars in a galaxy like ours, the Milky Way, you see the possibility. Furthermore, scientists now know that there are around a hundred billion galaxies. So, to the question of having a huge number of possibilities, the universe surely qualifies. Some people believe it's infinite. Now, when you start to use the "I" word, the scope of things goes to a whole new level.

My freshman algebra teacher at Smithtown High School West used an interesting example to try to help us understand the concept of infinity. He said that if you put a monkey at a typewriter and let it type for infinity… randomly hitting keys… that monkey would eventually type out the entire Encyclopedia Britannica, all 15 volumes! I can tell you it took a long while for me to accept that. I mean, what are the odds of randomly hitting keys to end up with just one sentence let alone a whole page… but a whole book… an encyclopedia?

Even today, scientists are still addressing this "monkey" problem. In *There is a God*, (HarperOne, 2007, pages 74–78) author Antony Flew summarizes a 2004 symposium presentation by Israeli scientist Gerald Schroeder. Schroeder calculated the probability of randomly typing one of Shakespeare's sonnets, "Shall I compare thee to a summer's day?" which contains 488 characters, to be 10 to the 609th power, or 1 with 690 zeroes behind it. This number is larger than the number of total particles (protons, electrons and neurons) in the universe, which is estimated to be 10 to the 80th power. Therefore, *in reality*, not even one Shakespearean sonnet could be produced by chance, much less the odds of producing the entire works of Shakespeare or an encyclopedia.

The key point to understand is that because my algebra teacher said the monkey typed for "infinity", that would mean that every conceivable combination of letters would emerge. *In theory*, the monkey would not only produce the entire Encyclopedia Britannica, it would reproduce every book ever written in English and every other language that uses our alphabet.

Even if the universe isn't infinite, it surely is massive and there must be innumerable planets similar to earth out there (although all stars to do not have planets). When the "base" of possibilities is large enough, even extremely unlikely things can occur. But what are the chances that life would spark and evolve out there? Without question, the chances are infinitesimally small. It takes just the right combination of facts and event then, we don't fully understand how it might happen. I suspect that it will remain the ultimate mystery for a long time but it's fascinating to consider the possibilities.

One branch of physics has postulated that there is really no such thing as time as we perceive it. I don't know about that, but I do believe we should live in the moment. Life truly is beautiful and so many people miss it because they're moving through it at breakneck speed. Others are so focused on what they perceive as the next, and more important life that they fail to appreciate the beauty that is all around them here and now. Few people would argue that the universe is wondrous and that, regardless of where it all came from, its existence is miraculous and we are very fortunate to be able to behold it.

Catalytic Concepts

- Science offers concrete evidence of how the world works on a day-to-day basis.
- Our lives and our careers dynamically interact with countless outside factors in a complex system (or set of systems).
- There is order within chaos and underlying systems provide the foundation and framework of life.
- We are born as a result of conception that carried with it millions of possibilities, yet we were created. Our lives continue to unfold with unlimited potential for diversity and beauty.
- Despite our deeply ingrained desire to do so, we cannot know the future; in fact, we can't even know all of the influences on the world, and on our lives and businesses in the present moment.
- We are a connected part of the universe and as such, its unlimited potential also resides within each one of us.

CHAPTER 11
Evidence in Business

"The key to success in merchandising is to put so much stuff out on the floor that just about anyone will find something they like."
–J. C. Penney

Business Building

Success in business is the result of planning, hard work, and competent execution. It's a many faceted and complicated thing in and of itself. There have been innumerable good books written and courses taught on the keys to business success and almost all of them have something useful to offer. In my own personal business experiences, I am a hard charging focused person who gets things done and I'm pretty good at encouraging other people to become involved in my "cause" and to lend support and best efforts to the goals of the team.

But I've always been aware of other factors influencing my triumphs and my tribulations. To me, because of the fact that it's a "virgin intellectual soil", it's fascinating to contemplate these outside influences and ponder the effects on our lives and businesses. I am not suggesting that these external factors are the keys to success, but I do want to highlight their existence and influence. Surely, outside influences play a role in the events that make up our business day, and ultimately, the business itself and it's an enlightened approach that allows rooms for them.

It's been said that knowledge is power, but the world of business is much more prone to interpretation than we might initially think. A major business "revelation" coming from the Enron debacle is that accounting can be manipulated to the benefit of top management. Now really, that's news? Accountants are humans, too (despite considerable evidence to the contrary) and much of the work is subjective. I remember early in my career as a CEO asking my first staff accountant, "What do the numbers show?" He replied, "What do you want them to show?" That was the beginning of my education on the subject and I found it even applied to outside accounting services. The practice of "shopping for an opinion" has been around for a very long time. NO, the operation of a business is not totally a world of precision (although the business of the business may call for extreme precision as in many kinds of manufacturing) and much is accomplished intuitively and by "guesstimate."

In some companies, the "leadership" provides direction much as the beautiful carved figures they used to put at the very front of sailing ships to lead the way. Even the simplest businesses function in a murky world where even internally, the left hand doesn't always know what the right hand is doing. Employees at many companies will tell you in confidence that the company succeeds in spite of itself and in spite of the management. Even when this is a widespread sentiment, the company may continue to make progress. Something is providing the impetus.

The captains of industry guide their companies to success using sophisticated strategic planning procedures. Part of leadership is creating the vision of a bright future which, when a whole lot of people buy into it, becomes a self-fulfilling prophecy. I can attest to the power of people in this regard. I can clearly remember specific circumstances of sharing my vision for the company with my team and having them take the dream and run with it and carry it through for "generations" of managers and making it a reality.

Established businesses have a major advantage in this area. Once a central "engine" of success is set up and functioning, maintenance is manageable and so is reaching out for incremental improvement (even in very large chunks). Occasionally, all the pieces fall into place, including the ones outside of anyone's control, and an enterprise will be able to churn out profits for a long time. You just replicate the established success over and over again. The company finds its niche (and nobody else does) and everyone lives happily ever after.

The Business Life Cycle

You have to be careful though, because there is growing evidenced that a business has a life cycle, too. Just in the brief span of my business career many once great companies, icons of American business, household names, have fallen. Companies like Kodak and Blockbuster. The most likely reason for their demise is change in the environment, in other words, outside influences. I don't think all of the people who were running those companies got stupid all at once. You see, it was an impossible task to actually know precisely what was making the company successful in the first place so when the "wind died down" nobody knew why.

Visionary leaders recognize that it's only a matter of time before the environment changes and so they step out of their comfort zone and seek new and different opportunities. It is like the process that Darwin observed in nature. As complicated organizations evolve, subtle changes emerge. Sometimes these are a variation on a theme, and sometimes they represent a whole new initiative. Variation sustains and strengthens over time; specialization weakens and eventually dies because the business environment will change. Although change can be painful, it is the hallmark of many successful organizations.

There are some outside influences beyond the scope of management's comprehension or control. Whenever we step out beyond the bounds of the success paradigm we know, it's very risky, indeed. The truth is a business, or businessperson, can never be certain of setting the right course of action, or making the correct decision until after the environment changes. It's the natural selection process. Changes in procedures, systems, products and other facets of business are evolving all the time. Some of those changes are well thought-out and proactive. Others simply occur. Then, the environment eventually changes. Everything that comes before is an educated guess at best. There is no "correct" answer before the changes in the environment because there is no way to accurately predict at the time what might evolve. Sometimes even the most well-thought-out efforts to improve can have dire consequences.

Opportunity Knocks

Outside influences create markets and opportunities, not business people. Astute business people find and capitalize on opportunities, but other forces make markets. It's very hard to identify a new market even when it already exists, let along predict or create them. But markets are the stuff of opportunity. Many established markets are well defined and well served and offer little real opportunity any more. The key questions relate to future markets and evolving tastes and trends. Who can account for the latest fashion in lifestyles, clothing, food, music, or television?

Many truly outstanding products, services, and technologies never find a market. This is common with new products that incorporate the latest technologies. Just because a product is capable of doing something, doesn't mean that people will recognize the need to do it. There may not be a market for it, especially if people have to modify their behavior in any way. Even when they do emerge and present themselves, markets are fickle. Sometimes they vanish as fast as they appear. Like so many other unexpected manifestations of natural beauty, some opportunities emerge but to un-noticed, underserved, and unrealized. They blossom, but no one sees them and they wither away.

A true opportunity is a rare and precious thing, and there are many people who have never been exposed to one—a real and significant one. It requires the alignment of many factors outside of our control. What we do with an opportunity is completely up to us but we are not responsible for creating opportunities. We can be proactive in our search, scanning the horizon. We should be actively seeking opportunity (and remember, it could be right in front of you), trying our own unique personal key in an attempt to unlock the potential in a situation, and in ourselves.

Opportunities are naturally occurring phenomena. They cannot be forced. You'll "feel it" when things are in alignment. There's a natural flow to it that can't be willed into an artificial opportunity. It's very possible to "try too hard," to attempt to create, rather than identify, markets and opportunities and that can have dire consequences.

The New Coke™

Perhaps one of the best "case studies" for this is the introduction of the "New Coke™" in 1985. Few products ever reach the levels of success that have been enjoyed by Coke™ over the last hundred years. From humble beginnings, Coke™ became an icon of our society that stood for decades. Coke™ created an industry. Though market share has slipped, it is still one of the great American business success stories on a global scale.

For decades, Coke™ was one of the most respected and best-run companies on the planet, widely appreciated as an outstanding strategic marketing company. Coke™ was sophisticated in their sales intelligence, advertising campaigns and distribution methodology.

However, in the early 1980's Coke™ was losing market share to Pepsi™, despite a massive advantage in marketing power. Roy Stout, head of market research for Coca-Cola™ USA, put it this way: "If we have twice as many vending machines, dominate fountains sales, have more shelf space, spend more on advertising, and are competitively priced—why are we losing share? You look at the Pepsi Challenge™, and you have to begin asking about taste."

Pepsi™ apparently tasted better to most people. So, in a bold move, the top management at Coke™ began a lengthy and expensive project to reformulate the world's most successful soft drink to bring its taste up to speed with the times. Millions of dollars were spent tweaking the formula. Over 200,000 blind taste tests were conducted and in test after test, people preferred the New Coke™ over the original formula and over Pepsi™. This was all done by a bunch of very smart people who knew their business inside and out and had almost unlimited resources at their disposal to ensure they were making the right decisions. The introduction of the New Coke™ was said to have been one of the most thoroughly researched product introductions in history. It was going to be a slam-dunk.

With incredible fanfare, marketing and advertising support, the New Coke™ was introduced in the Spring of 1985. It bombed.

Despite tons of evidence to the contrary, consumers didn't like it or didn't want it or whatever. To this day no one has been able to explain it. Embarrassed and humiliated, Coke™ reintroduced its original formula a couple of months later.

Needless to say, this is one (dramatic) example of something that happens all of the time in business. Business is largely about trial and error. It's not my point here to analyze all that went wrong with the new Coke™. But, here's the "take away"; no matter how much you do a test, research, and analyze a decision; no matter how certain you are before you "press the button," you can rest assured—some elements of the situation are not evident to you. You are unable to take them into consideration because you do not perceive them. The best we can hope for is a well-educated guess. Outside influences will always be present. Always. That you can know for sure, you just can't know what their effects will be.

Usually, their presence is inconsequential. Occasionally they "turn up the heat" and make their presence known. Sometimes their effect is very positive. A business can flourish or an unlikely product can be a smash hit (remember the Fidget Spinner?). Trends can emerge, blossom, whither, and die—all baffling the "experts". Sometimes a product can both blossom and whither within a short time span.

The Financial Future

A past Chairman of the Security Exchange Commission, Harvey Pitt, commented in a television interview about the efficacy of the business analysts employed by the Wall Street brokerage houses. These are people who are paid huge incomes (in some cases in excess of millions of dollars a year) to analyze public companies, their circumstances, their financials, their management, and their potential for ongoing success. They are supposedly gurus who have an uncanny ability to predict the future of businesses and industries. These are the people, for the most part, who precipitated the dot-come craze in the mid-nineties. All of their analysis is supposed to boil down to a general idea of where the stock price of a particular company is going. Pitt's comment? "Business analysts are very good at looking at what's happened in a company in the past. They can also evaluate the general health of a company today, in the present. They are not too good at predicting the future of stock prices. In that, they are pretty unreliable." No kidding? Do you have any idea how much money somebody could make if they could consistently predict stock prices (up or down) with even a moderate degree of accuracy?

Professor William Gehring of the University of Michigan has done extensive research on the science of the brain. Gehring and his colleagues drew their conclusions by using and EEG to monitor brain waves of many subjects as they were exposed to various situations in different experiments. The findings were recently published in the journal *Science*. "Economists assume that people are rational about their decisions and the economy works in this rational fashion," he said. "We now know there are lots of situations where people make decisions based on false assumptions and expectations."

Truth is, even the best and the brightest are making an educated guess and almost always our information is flawed and/or incomplete. (Have you ever said, "If I had known THAT, I would have done things differently"?) In most situations, there are factors involved beyond anyone's comprehension.

Yet the huge "industry" that emerged around financial news and financial analysis, designed to guide investors, is a multi-billion-dollar industry in and of itself. All of the big brokerage houses have business analysts who look closely at the stock market and the performance of public companies. Economists study the economy and draw conclusions about its direction. Literally thousands of really bright, highly educated people spend the better part of their waking hours developing an understanding of financial markets. Now remember, the rewards for getting this right are massive! It's not like these people are blasé about it. They work extremely hard and regularly put their reputation on the line… and about half the time, they get it wrong.

In fact, the *Wall Street Journal* regularly ran a contest every year (I'm not sure if they still do it or not). Here's how it worked: They would get five professional money managers to pick one stock each January 1st. There were no restrictions; they could pick any public stock they wanted. And they only had to pick one stock.

Now, if you were a professional money manager and all you did was analyze stocks, don't you think you'd be able to pick at least one stock that would go up in the new year? Doesn't seem too hard, right? It might be hard to pick ten that would go up, but one?

Now in addition to the five professional money managers, the Journal staff would pin the daily stock listing to the wall, and throw five darts at it from about 25 feet away (so no one could aim). The darts would randomly "pick" five stocks and the money managers picked five stocks and they would track all ten through the course of the year.

Guess what? By a slight margin of victory, the stocks picked by throwing darts beat the stocks picked by the professional money managers. Sometimes people "over-think" things. The darts were totally random.

This demonstrates "doublethink" at its best. Here's an entire industry of very smart people who go to work each day putting their considerable efforts into something that they know is pretty much impossible to do. In fact, if you pay close attention to the financial media, you'll innumerable slight references, usually humorous, to this paradox. Then they quickly get back on point and act like they know what's going on. It's their mokita. It doesn't help when the publication that is the heart of the industry demonstrates the futility of their efforts with a dart contest.

One television show added insult to injury. They stacked one professional money manager up against, can you believe this, a chimpanzee. The pro picked some stocks and the monkey, using a red marker and a list of randomly picked the same number. The outcome? The money manager said, "I guess I need to eat more bananas." Of course, the chimp represented randomness, but it was still very embarrassing.

Analysis has its place but we often "play a hunch" and rely on our intuition or a gut feel. Effective management, investing, and success in business is often a blend of both.

Don't Take Information Too Seriously

This all makes for some good-natured fun but I think there's a much bigger, more important point here. For all the charts, grids, economic theories, intense study and analysis, the stock market and the economy are just too complicated to fully comprehend. Yet, human nature being what it is, we continue to try to understand it (as we should). We read the *Journal, Forbes, Fortune, Investor's Business Daily* and *Money*. CNBC presents us with around the clock financial analysis (I love watching Squawk Box in the morning—heck, I was featured on Squawk Box). To some degree, that's like daily reports on the growth of a tree, but it's still entertaining. We micro-analyze every subtle aspect of every company action. We project company performance, and then compare actual results to projections, all in an attempt to predict the future. Talk with veterans of the game and they will tell you, to a person, it's a very tough to get it right. Through all the analysis, stock prices rise and fall, oftentimes inexplicably.

It makes all the sense in the world to learn as much as possible before investing, but you should never put all of your eggs in one basket. Natural selection, complexity theory, and outside influences seem to dictate that there is only one effective strategy for investing; diversification tempered with realistic expectations.

Drilling for Oil

In the early years of the oil industry, finding oil was part science, part intuition, part experience, and a lot of luck. Modern technology has broken the code and removed much of the risk, but it was highly speculative in the beginning. As with mining for precious metals, lots of people went broke looking for that gusher that would make them rich. All kinds of methods were used to detect the presence of black gold but oftentimes efforts resulted in a dry well. The oil wells that "hit" made millionaires.

In many ways, starting a new business today is like drilling for oil back before radar and ultra-sound. You're trying to tap into an unrecognized resource… trying to identify a market, a product, a need, or interest that is not being served, or could be better served. The old prospector could not know for sure what was below the surface, and neither can you. But starting a new business usually is much more complicated than finding oil because so many factors are involved.

This is the essential realization behind the strategy of acquisition versus launching a new business. When you look at all the challenges associated with buying a company, blending cultures, policies, products and programs, and you see the dismal record corporations have in making mergers or acquisitions work, you wonder why anyone would do it. It's simple, there's a working business in place (even if it has a lot of room for improvement) and since the record for starting a business from scratch is even more dismal, a functioning business has inherent value. The value is in the original creative process of breathing life into an idea. The care and feeding and nurturing of a fledging business, otherwise known as the practice of management, comes after the inception. It's like starting a fire; it's tricky sometimes to get it going. Once it is well lit, you can just throw in another log and tend it from time to time.

The Key to Business Success

Over the years I've worked with lots of people that have achieved many different levels of success. Most recently our Internet Mastery Community has generated tens of millions of dollars in sales on Amazon. The results speak for themselves. When I get together with people who have started and grown their online business, I'll often ask them the following question: "What is the key to the success you have achieved so far?" It's a fascinating exercise and yields some very interesting insights into human nature and the nature of business and management.

Over the years, I have asked this question of thousands of workshop attendees in over 100 cities and more than 10 countries. The setting is almost always private and serious. People understand the importance of the question and the work to provide me with good information about the dynamics of the success and results they have achieved. The experience is consistent… the answers are always different. Within an online business there are specific tasks that are completed on a daily basis but they see the key to their success as many different things. Now, of course, there will also be some consistency as you may well imagine, but more often than not the differences are stark and sometimes controversial. Remember, this question is retrospective. We're not asking, "Where do you think the future direction of the business should be headed?" You could understand some differences of opinion about future plans, but this question focused on the historic strengths of the business. They all attended the same initial Internet Mastery workshop. They all are selling on Amazon (in this example). They all had coaches and learned the same system yet the way they do the business is varies. And, so does their results.

What does this tell us about our understanding of the dynamics of having online business success if the people doing the business see the success of their business in very different yet plausible ways? It tells us that perceptions vary greatly and that it's very difficult if not impossible to truly understand "where the wind is coming from" in business success.

Earlier I touched upon the question of perception versus reality. We tend to want to keep that question among our philosophical playthings and don't think about its implications for the business world, but they are very real. The April 1, 2002 issue of *Business Week* magazine had an interesting cover story entitled, "Restating the '90s." Using sophisticated analysis, author Michael Mandel highlighted some fascinated conclusions.

You remember the 90's, right? It was a time of explosive growth. 401k plans grew dramatically. People got into investing in a big way. It was called the largest single legal creation of wealth in history. Guess what? The '80s were better. Take a look at some of Mandel's findings:

PERCEPTION: Investors did better in the 1990s than in the 1980s.
REALITY: Workers received 99% of the gains from faster productivity growth at non-financial corporations (compensation rose faster than at any other time since the 1950s).
PERCEPTION: Technology hurt low-skill workers.
REALITY: Blue-collar and service workers saw real wages rise sharply in the tech-driven 1990s.

PERCEPTION: 401k Plans and retirement plans grew at a record pace due to the influx of dot com initial public offerings.

REALITY: The stock market crash in the late 1990's wiped out fortunes virtually overnight.

To a student of business, Mandel's findings set a whole decade on its head. Clearly, our universal perceptions on the subject were off-target. Some things defy logic and understanding. Now any well-run business has a body of knowledge that is certain and understood, especially long-established ones. But in many there are dynamic forces at work, particularly in the marketplace, that you may not be aware of or fully comprehend. Surely, for all businesses, there are significant outside influences, starting with the (often fickle) market itself, which we respond to, but don't create.

The Illusion of Control

"Control" is a key concept in business management. A person or persons can have total internal control of a very small, simple enterprise. But beyond that, it's largely an illusion. There is no such thing as total control in business. Power, like life itself, is temporarily granted and can be revoked quickly and unmercifully. Outside influences can blitzkrieg your business and turn your world upside down. And, it can have an incredibly positive set of results.

Many well-run businesses, invincible in most aspects of their operation, have an Achilles' heal—a small point of vulnerability. It could come from a competitor that's planning an assault. It could come from something you're remotely aware of or from your blind side. It could be anything from changing market conditions to governmental intervention. The power of business is usually trumped by the power of government. If some bureaucrat in Washington decides to make trouble for you or your industry, batten down the hatches.

For employees, this is even truer because you are dependent, to an extent, on the people at the top. Unfortunately, they are much more prone to reigning down torture and indiscriminate pain than to benevolent action, which could actually benefit you and your family. The "Us" and "Them" mentality that exists at most companies is the result of careful observation and experience, not automatic rejection of authority. The rank and file "flinch" reflexively when another corporate communication comes their way because it usually means more job cuts (so the same amount of work must now be done by fewer employees) or other belt tightening. Worse yet, it might be to announce that the company's been acquired so even if an employee is doing a good job, they might get a new boss that doesn't agree. The reality of outside influences is acute for people lower on the totem pole.

As the economy expands, voids are created and demand sucks certain products and services to extraordinary heights. A company must be poised to take advantage of these emerging opportunities and management must effectively deploy resources and inspire extraordinary efforts from their team. Many opportunities come into existence and subsequently evaporate because no one perceives them or is prepared to take advantage of them.

Business is, and always will be, the providence of the aggressive, professional, focused, smart, driven individual. By paying careful attention to team dynamics, market analysis, training, compensation, recognition and strategic analysis, managers can prepare their companies for success. But also by recognizing the influence of outside factors, you will fortify your enterprise and minimize the chances of external elements thwarting your progress and reducing your success.

 Catalytic Concepts

- Business success is based primarily on the traditional factors of management, leadership, competence, execution and a commitment to excellence.
- Business is also subject to many outside influences and unknown factors.
- We seek even greater control in the business environment than we do in our personal lives. A limited amount of control is available to some people in an organization, but other factors will intrude.
- It may be difficult to pinpoint the central reasons for a business to fail or succeed. It's often hidden even from individuals intimately familiar with the inner workings of a company.

- Established businesses can replicate success, often for many years, but may be in an inevitable business life cycle.
- Innovation can be fostered but is also random, as it is in nature.
- Extremely well researched initiatives can sometimes fail due to unforeseen influences. Complexity can render attempts at understanding futility.
- An established business has overcome the challenges of inception and has an inherent value by virtue of its existence and early success as an enterprise.
- The known dynamics of business success are well documented but there is also a hidden mysterious side of the equation.

CHAPTER 12
Acceptance

"It is one thing to show a man that there is an error, and another to put him in possession of the truth."

–John Locke

A Sense of Knowing

The value to you accepting and understanding outside influences could be enormous but it will take time. At the minimum, there's a sense of wonder than can evolve into awareness. It elevates you above the ruckus; gives you a better perspective on what's happening around you. It is delightful to watch life unfold once you understand the beauty of its randomness. Of course, knowledge is power and when combined with action, a person who understands the underlying dynamics of success is far better suited to achieve it. An understanding of outside influences makes you aware that success can never be guaranteed. But, you will have a competitive advantage because you understand that they affect your life and you'll better able to get them working in your favor.

We've all heard the phrase "Timing is everything." Timing is a key outside influence. We're talking about the relationship of our decisions and actions as they interact with dynamic factors beyond our control. "When" you buy a particular stock matters greatly. Almost all stocks were a good investment at some point in time. In a sense, "when" matters more than "what" stock you buy as they all tend to fluctuate in value.

Just recently I watched Amazon stock drop 35% in less than 3 weeks. With that said, Amazon stock was up 100% in the previous 12 months. If you purchased the stock at the high price, before the drop, you would have lost a lot of money (if you sold the shares). If you purchased in the year previous, you would have been up more than 50%. Amazon is a great stock but the timing of when you purchased it matters.

Timing isn't everything but it sure is important. And it's largely out of our control in our lives, starting at the beginning of our lives. We do not control the timing of our birth, and pretty much all other major "timing" in our life plays off of that. When we start school is a function of when we were born. We have some control over when we enter the workforce but not over the career environment when we do so. The complex machinery of the world is very much established and all in full motion and operation when we "drop in".

Now, we still control most of what happens as we navigate along, playing the cards we are dealt. But life is not unilateral; it's the intricate interaction of the things within our control and the outside influences which come to bear that yields up that string of experiences, relationships, successes and failures we call life.

Hopefully, after considering the evidence presented, you can see the pervasive presence of outside influences that subtly affect almost every aspect of our lives. Acceptance does not come easy. It will take time. Biologist P.B. Medawar noted, "The human mind treats new ideas the way the body treats a strange protein; it rejects it." What you previously believed about how success occurs has been a part of the way you viewed the world for a long time. And, don't forget, you've got to employ doublethink because the point of this book is not that life just happens to you as you go along for the ride, but that you make life happen. My point is that many outside influences are being exerted on your life but you still must accept personal responsibility for your actions and decisions within that context. Many people are dealt great cards and squander them along the way. Others turn a bad hand into a winning hand with adroit play and many other positive traits. Outside influences come to the rescue of some and bulldoze others.

There are some events in life that are so obviously outside of our control that there is no plausible argument to be made otherwise. They happen as a result of random factors of timing and inconsequential decisions that lead to major life outcomes. Our conception, as opposed to one of the other millions of people who could have resulted at that moment, is one of those. Some might ask why this is even important. The answer is that it's a glimpse of a system that continues to revolve around us and involve many aspects of our lives. Randomness doesn't end at conception and we are much better prepared for life when we acknowledge and attempt to understand it.

Some people don't want to face that reality. I do understand their reluctance, but it doesn't change the facts. You are not totally in control of your destiny. You are not totally responsible for your success, mediocrity, or failure. A straight shooter, President Harry Truman acquired the catch phrase, "Give 'em hell, Harry" to which he is said to have replied, "I don't give 'em hell. I just tell 'em the truth and they think it is hell." Sometimes the truth does hurt but we need to hear it. Interestingly, in the case of outside influences, understanding it will eventually relieve some pain caused by the common misconceptions about success. Observation of the phenomenon and its effects on things will lead to understanding, appreciation and comfort.

Strive for Excellence and Honor Effort

One of the keys to satisfaction and fulfillment is to remember the age-old truth and correlate it to outside influences. The key is in the beauty of productive work with the nobility of striving for our best effort. This is why it's so important to find work that is meaningful and enjoyable for you. If the paycheck is secondary, still important, but not *the* reason for showing up on Monday morning, then you've got your priorities straight. Obviously (unfortunately?) there is such a thing as money and such things as bills, but perhaps we can still learn to look to the work we do and the beauty of each day for satisfaction.

You know what they say, "It's not whether you win or lose, it's how you play the game." Of course it's not whether you win or lose because outside influences may determine that. When that old phrase was coined a long time ago, people intuitively understood that the "zero sum" approach (one team wins and one team loses) to most sports makes it necessary to focus on the valiant effort of the players as what really counts. We've all seen, or been part of, a particularly had fought sporting event where everybody says, "It seems a shame that one team had to lose, they all played their hearts out." These are the tough losses because in terms of the ebb and flow of the game, it's very possible both teams played equally well. Unfortunately, unless it's a tie, the scoreboard has to reflect a winner and a loser. Conflict arises from this because, somehow, everyone involved in the game—the players, coaches, and fans—everyone knows that both teams played equally well. But the concepts of winning and losing run deep and, at the end, one team walks away jubilant, the other team with their heads down and tears rolling down their cheeks. You see this in politics as well as other facets of life where competition is involved.

Despite the multitude of factors that determine who wins a sporting event, sports are extremely simple compared to the complexities of life and business. This simplicity lends itself to the idea of winners and losers. Scorekeeping is far from a perfect science and oftentimes a team with more talent can lose a game due to some quirk or crazy play, even a bad call by a referee or umpire; but at least, at the end of the game, you can look at the scoreboard and have a sense of finality.

Life, on the other hand, hopefully goes on for a long while for all of us. It is much harder off the field or court to determine the score. But this leads to an important conclusion regarding accomplishment and achievement. To strive for excellence for the sake of excellence is one of the keys to a satisfying life. It's a wonderful feeling to do something well, and our society does not put enough emphasis on that fact. In this aspect of life, it's not about pleasing someone else. It's about finding something we like to do, and doing it well, even if it's not a lucrative activity.

We must always keep working to be our best. It's the key to personal satisfaction and personal growth. We must "try" for success and happiness, for without trying, success cannot occur. It is important to learn to appreciate the effort and draw satisfaction from a job well done. There is little satisfaction from acquired "success" without the accompanying hard work. It's working for something and achieving it that brings the glow. That's why people who win big lottery payoffs report hollow feelings down the road. I'm not saying they want to give the money back (although studies have shown that many go through it quickly and return to their former lifestyle) but just that "something's missing." The thing that is missing is the effort that produces the benefit.

The quest for success will always lead to frustration for the majority of us if it is a comparative or competitive thing. By definition, the top one percent of one percent is a very small group (in all of America about 30,000 people). Only a few can be at the very top of the "standings." If that's your criterion for success, well I hope you make it. If success is internal, judging from the quality of our effort, then we can find satisfaction regardless of the "scoreboard." It is the effort that elevates a person above the ordinary. Character in action, quality of effort, and the integrity of our activity—these are what matter in the long run. Furthermore, we should learn to see this in others and "honor the effort" that they put forth as well.

Vince Lombardi said, "Fatigue makes cowards out of us all." In other words, it takes courage to move forward and make the effort when we're tired, weak and beaten. It takes courage to face life's challenges with dignity and resolve, to not turn away. Especially when you understand that outside influences could have an effect on the outcome of your work. It is at this point where inspirational speaker Dr. Eric Thomas would say you have to "grind".

Think about it, whom do you respect and for what reasons? At the end of the day, it's those who are true to themselves and their ideals that earn our respect. The person who is big enough to treat everyone with honor and dignity is the person we most admire. In the final analysis, how much money a person earns or has accumulated is not necessarily a very good measure of that person.

Courage, Character, and Noble Motivations

One of my favorite movies is *Braveheart*. In the character of William Wallace, Mel Gibson exemplified this point beautifully. The William Wallace of *Braveheart* was a true leader and a true hero. His approach to leadership was simple and eloquent, "Follow me." My definition of a leader is a person who gets voluntary support of followers, whom the leader inspires to great efforts (in a worthy cause). Great leaders "wick out" the enthusiasm, efforts and commitment of their followers. People are drawn to a worthy cause. William Wallace was motivated by a desire for the freedom and security of his people; he led by example and they followed him willingly against incredible odds. He rebelled against the tyranny of English rule. He gave his life for his quest and defied the English to his last breath.

Now if you've seen the movie, you know that the antagonist was the English King, "Longshankes." He was motivated by greed and the lust for power. He led by fear and manipulation. Although he was very rich and powerful (he was "royalty" after all) he was a loathsome character. This classic tale shows us much about the proper way to conduct our lives.

Outside influences teaches us that we must honor the effort because we can never sure of the outcome. Looking back on a job well done can be, should be, a satisfying, fulfilling experience. If it should yield quantifiable financial benefits, that's wonderful. If it doesn't, this perspective still provides a framework for appreciation of what you accomplished and a sense of satisfaction.

And the hero must bear witness to the struggle that we all wage every moment of our lives. In which there are no happy endings because there is no end. And like Prometheus must remind us that the struggle is heroic.
–Diane Tittle Delott

The Big Time

Humility is a scarce and noble character trait. In our society of "in your face" wealth and conspicuous consumption it has become accepted that "greed is good." Did you see the movie *"The Wolf of Wall Street"*? When you in inject the effect of outside influences into the equation, it will help keep things in perspective. If you've made it big time remember that good fortune has shined upon you. Sure you've worked hard, but so have those less fortunate. Certainly, you're bright and talented, but so is the rank and file. Of course, you've contributed mightily, and so have many, many others.

Even when things are going extraordinarily well, resist the temptation to build the false conclusion that you are somewhere a more-worthy human being, because "it just ain't so." Graciously accept the bounty and be gentle in your interactions with others. There is a big difference between power and force. True power does not force the issue. It is a sign of inner strength to be compassionate and demonstrate empathy. The best way to get genuine respect is to give it; it cannot be bought or paid for. The best way to be revered is to treat everyone with reverence. It is not a sign of weakness to show gratitude. Shine the light back at your comrades in the fight and find ways to share with them (and not just the limelight). Acknowledge everyone else's efforts and they will acknowledge yours. But also know quietly within, that outside influences have been an unmistakable factor in your success as well.

The Arrogance of Influence

The alternative path to the humble, gracious, generous one is the self-centered arrogant one. This is the one usually chosen by weaker people. There are a few gaps in nature (with the possible exception of the Grand Canyon) that are as large and wide as the gap between the self-perceived importance of one of these successful people (especially a middle-aged white male like me) and their actual importance to society. The human ability to develop an egocentric view of the world is truly mind-boggling and it goes up exponentially as net worth rises. Many doctors in America optimize this self-aggrandizement as they discount the value of their patients' time (and therefore the value of the lives of their patients) by filling waiting rooms and elongating waiting periods to maximize the efficiency of the doctor's own day.

When your life has led to abundance and you want to take all the credit for that yourself, you've got a tricky path to navigate. A lot of energy must go into maintaining a certain status quo, for others, and for you. Caught up in the pseudo drama of looking, acting, and feeling self-important, the "kings and queens" of business parade down the street naked and everyone proclaims how beautiful their new clothes are.

It takes an extraordinary person to practice humility as former Israeli Prime Minister Golda Meir (1898-1978) noted in admonishing, "Don't be humble. You're not that great."

Every once in a while, an executive comes along who breaks the mold and almost always, that person is revered for it. Sam Walton drove an old pickup truck because it got him where he needed to go. His massive wealth (he was one of the first billionaires in the world) did not go to his head. He never forgot the "little people" that contributed so mightily to his business success.

The path to maturity runs from the infant who is self-centered to the fully evolved adult who is totally outward in their view of the world. A genuine, caring, giving person who lives life to serve and help others has transcended the childish pursuit of self-aggrandizement. There is a tremendous lack of maturity that exists in the world today. The fully evolved mature person moves quietly through life, and doesn't need constant reinforcement, or to be the center of attention. Unfortunately, there are very few of these highly evolved creatures walking on the planet.

You can be one of them. If you have met with a great deal of success in your life, be sure not to walk around thinking you're God's gift to your company (or the world at large). Have humility and demonstrate generosity. Remember the caveat, "there, but for the grace of God, go I." I don't think God makes decisions about who will be affluent and who will be poor. What is meant there is that forces outside of our control could have been, or yet could be, exerted to make a big difference in where we end up in life. Those forces are there, to be sure, and once we acknowledge them it puts a slightly different slant on just about everything. Being grateful for success, and gracious and humble in our interactions, is far superior to an arrogant self-centered approach to life.

Room to Grow

Chances are, on the other hand, you still seek success and excellence in your life. You may have felt the frustration of doing things right, and doing all the right things, only to find that success has eluded you. I can't tell you how many people

I've spoken to through the years who simply can't figure out how it is they aren't where they planned to be or hoped to be. These are bright, hard-working, well-educated people and they've followed the prescribed path only to find that it did not lead to the "promised land." They got their degree(s) and went to work for the right companies. They have a very strong desire for success, yet it's remained just outside of their grasp.

This wreaks havoc on their self-esteem and self-worth… and it shouldn't. If you haven't quite met with the success you've hoped for in your life, stop "flogging" yourself. In all likelihood, you're a good and talented person who has gotten some bad breaks along the way. It's great to keep in mind that the pattern can and often does change. Many people struggle for success for decades before they get things properly aligned.

Perhaps you caught part of the wonderful documentary produced by the Discovery channel called *The Blue Planet*. It focused on our oceans and the phenomenal abundance of life they support. One dramatic scene was a metaphor for the point I'm making here. It focused on a huge flock of penguins trying to get up onto a rocky island. The island had no beach, just a stone cliff some ten to fifteen feet above the water line. The penguins needed to ride the waves in as the swells crashed against the rocks. At the peak of the ride, the sea birds would launch themselves forward and hopefully land on top of the rocky plateau.

It was a brutal scene as many made it, and many didn't. The ones that didn't often got stuck on a ledge on the face of the cliffs and were then smashed by subsequent incoming waves. They fell down in crevasses and got badly beaten up if they didn't land on the ledge. Now, to a human being, all penguins sure look alike. My guess is they all are pretty much alike in "personality" and "intelligence" and "skill." I think the ones that "made it" were not necessarily any smarter, any stronger, or any more "talented" than the ones who didn't, but they sure were a whole lot better off. Watching their behavior as they waited for the waves, they were all acting pretty much the same way. Waves are, of course, very random with no two being exactly the same. They just randomly caught the right wave at the right time.

It was interesting that, once they did land up top, the penguins just went about their business. They didn't rejoice and applaud their successes. They didn't bemoan or belittle the ones that didn't make it. Getting up onto the island was just part of life to them. Most eventually made it. Some didn't.

If you haven't hit it big yet, appreciate yourself and your efforts. Perhaps the next wave is yours. There are some ways to increase your changes that I'll highlight in the next chapter. In the meantime, "honor the effort" that you put forth each day. Give your best for the sake of doing so and for the personal satisfaction you will feel. Value yourself as a meaningful important person and don't allow the scales created by others to measure your success.

Blending

The human desire for a simple "step-by-step" approach to success runs deep. There is no shortage of success literature. Many authors and success gurus have attempted to fill that need. The problem is life just isn't that simple and cannot be broken down into a few easy steps despite our desire and considerable effort. You can't simply take charge and follow the high performance habbits of successful people. Reading a manifesto on motivation isn't the answer. What's called for is a blended approach that considers the traditional principles of attaining success but also acknowledges outside influences.

We all know what like to (or need to) think: get a good education, acquire the knowledge and skills we need, work hard with honesty and integrity, manage your money properly, and you're on the path to success. Well, that is partially right. But to ignore the effects of outside factors beyond our control is like fighting a battle with only partial knowledge of, or worse, a misconception of the enemy. By now I'm sure you see the widespread influence of many external factors that will influence your life. They are real and they will make themselves known to you, one way or another.

To some degree, knowledge of outside influences doesn't require you to take any action. It contributes to your edification and evolution. This book is not just about gaining more success, although more success will be in your future. This book is also about appreciating a dynamic force in life that affects all of us. It's about understanding and coming to peace with some of the contradictions that are so apparent in life. So that, when the idiosyncrasies of the system manifest themselves, you'll be able to understand what's happening and appreciate the bounty or cope with the challenges.

But, with outside influences as a backdrop, I want to re-emphasize a point I've made several times already; you still are the single largest factor in determining the level of success in your life. You are the key and most critical influence. A thorough knowledge of outside influences further expands your chances of success in conjunction with hard work, a good education, having a mentor or a coach and all the components of the well-worn traditional approach.

 **Catalytic Concepts**

- Understanding the ideas behind outside influences provides a framework for a sense of knowing, and appreciation for the dynamic external forces that affect our lives and businesses.
- There is tremendous value in a philosophy about life and work that "honors the effort" we put forth each day. We elevate our work and our lives by the approach we take daily.
- Knowledge of the influence of factors beyond our control provides us some guidance in how to conduct ourselves. Those who have attained success should practice generosity, moderation and humility, and gain respectability by being respectful of others.
- The courageous, engaged leader shuns the trappings of success in favor of a fully integrated and available style.
- Those that have not yet achieved their goals should not diminish or devalue themselves or their contributions and ideas. Self-worth and self-esteem are appropriate for all because we all possess beauty and value.
- Blending the understanding of outside influences with the time honored steps of success increases the odds in our favor of achieving breakthrough accomplishments in our lives. Knowledge is power.

CHAPTER 13

Be Open to the Universe

"If the doors of perception were cleansed everything would appear to man as it is, infinite."

–William Blake

Opportunity Abounds

Y ou can never know when all of the pieces will come together and success will bloom all around you. Your hard work synchronizes with outside influences and it's like a booster rocket that propels you forward. One thing is for certain; there is more opportunity today than ever before. Markets continue to emerge, flourish and grow. Quality of life continues as Americans have demonstrated at an insatiable desire for anything that can make life easier, more comfortable or more fun. Explosions of creativity and innovation yields fortunes to the people at the source. Human endeavor is at its highest level of accomplishment, and despite tragic examples of our barbaric side, the world blossoms with the beauty of human achievement. The last fifty years in America have been, without question, the golden years of human life on this planet. Nothing that existed before comes close.

Technology opens up whole new worlds. In fact, here's a little secret about the Internet: We were not wrong about its potential for revolutionizing commerce and communications in the mid 1990's, we were just wrong on the timing. We demonstrated one of our American weaknesses, impatience. We want everything now. We didn't want to wait. In our "irrational exuberance" we ignored the learning curve. Watch business opportunities continue to evolve in the Internet. More opportunity will emerge for those ready to explore the possibilities and willing to understand that it takes time to grow a business. The Internet today has created the greatest opportunities for growth and income in the history of business. It's here now.

Opportunity is everywhere. But how do you know that an opportunity is right for you? What are the criteria for judging whether or not something will yield success from your hard work? Part of what prepared me to bring these ideas out is that I've been both at the top and at the bottom. I've had tremendous successes and I've also futilely banged my head against the wall trying to make something work that never did. As I studied my successes and failures, I had to acknowledge that I brought the same skills and talents (such as they are) to each thing that I tried. I worked just as hard at each but had very different results. Truth is, I cannot be sure, even in retrospect why some things failed and some succeeded. I can develop some very plausible partial explanations but I can't say totally and for certain. Fortunately, the ability to fully and completely understand one's success is not a prerequisite for achieving it; otherwise we'd have a lot fewer millionaires (and even billionaires) in the world. If you look real close and don't overcomplicate the issue, you can find one common thread in the many tapestries of success.

A Basketball Contest

Earlier I referenced Lebron James, but Michael Jordan is arguably considered the greatest basketball history in the history of the game. In 2002 after a lay-off of several years subsequent to his first return, Jordan (39) left the front office of the Washington Wizards and went onto the court as team captain. Make no mistake about this, if you had the privilege of seeing Michael Jordan play basketball, you have seen one of the greatest athletes of all time—period. Despite the fact that he showed only flashes of his prior brilliance, he received more votes than any other player during that year for the NBA All-Star Game.

To make a point here, I want to set up an imaginary "basketball" contest and make Michael Jordon one of the contestants. Let's say the other contestant is a 65-year-old woman, 4' 11" tall, who has never played basketball in her life. I don't think I'd have to ask you whom you would pick in a basketball contest between these two people. Now, before you answer, let me tell you a little bit more about this imaginary contest and the rules I have in mind.

Since obviously Michael Jordan would be totally dominant physically, the contest would not be a one-on-one game of basketball. The contest would be to see who would make the most foul shots or free throws. Still want Michael Jordan? I don't blame you.

Oh, there's one other little thing I neglected to mention about the contest. We're going to give Michael Jordan ten free throw shots and "Granny," our other contestant will get 10,000 shots. Now, the question is, who do you think would make the most free throws? I think it's safe to say that Michael Jordan would make eight, nine or perhaps ten for ten. But I also think that a person with no prior basketball experience or any obvious skill is likely to make at least eleven out of the 10,000 shots.

That little imaginary contest speaks to the point I want to make here. You see, life has been very generous to us. Life is aware of the effects of outside influences so it hasn't limited us to just ten chances or even just 10,000 chances. Life has said, try as often as you like. In addition, we get the added guaranteed benefits of many wonderful experiences as a bonus. Experience is its own reward sometimes.

Try Lots of Things

There is one thing, and only one thing, that can be said about ALL successful people… they tried something. Probably they tried many things. Trying is the universal constant at the initiation of success. It is the ticket to get into the game. After all, it's hard to find anything that applies to them all. Most work really hard for sure. But so do a lot of people who've never hit it big or even come close. Hard work is just not the determining factor. It is a prerequisite, but hard work alone will not distinguish you from the pack. Lots of hard-working people die broke. Trying is the core of every success that's ever been achieved. It's one of the secrets of the universe that there's no limit to the number of things that we can try. What an exciting idea.

Failing to learn from nature (remember massive effort), oftentimes we try something once, don't get the desired result, and give up. Few things have as much effect on our overall success as our willingness to try and to be open to new possibilities. Getting in the game is the first step to becoming an All-Star. Remember, in competition to become a success, lots of people are already in the game. Somebody's going to hit the goal. It's impossible to say who will, but we do know for certain who won't… those who never try. It's your time to try—and you should do it now.

George Bernard Shaw said, "I've failed at nine out of ten things I've tried in my life." The fact of the matter is, if we were to evaluate objectively and recollect completely, that statement is true for the majority of us. Successful businesses are always trying and testing new products and new ideas. Successful people do, too. I know that I've certainly tried lots of things and there are many advantages to doing so.

First of all, every new experience, regardless of whether or not it is a "success," brings experiential value. There will be value in the people that you meet. There will most likely be value in the things you'll learn. Truly I've learned as much in some of the failures that I've had as I've learned from some of my successes. Both yield learnings if you look for them.

The other part of this that speaks directly to the concept of outside influences is that, regardless of how in-depth your analysis may be, you'll never know for certain whether something will or will not work for you until you try it. Just because it works for some people doesn't mean that it will work for all people. And if It's new and innovative, there's even less to go on in making your evaluation. You've read this point several times already in this book.

Waste is a terrible thing. We think about this in our day-to-day lives and try not to waste food, or waste gasoline, or waste money. But the truth is some people waste something far more precious. Inside of each of us there is a fountain of talent and ability, some of it, probably most of it, untapped (and thus wasted) in most people. It is so true that you are your own worst critic. We constantly under-value our potential and ourselves. Even the things we do attempt, we seldom give our best for fear of failure. What if there was not failure, only degrees of success. Many more people would try many more things, and examples of genius would occur all around us.

Search for the Spark

There's an intangible "spark" when a person puts himself or herself into a good business situation, career move or other circumstance. That spark lets you know you're in the right place at the right time. And sometimes it can take many, many tries before you hit one that "lights your fire." It's hard to identify what creates it but it's the kind of thing that you know when you find it. It's largely beyond our control. We contribute part of the equation and outside influences provide the rest. Just as in affairs of the heart, most great careers or great businesses begin as love stories. Loving your work minimizes the importance of financial reward you gain from it, and increases your chances for success.

You never know when the "spark" will occur. So, employing the concepts behind *"Outside Influences"* clearly dictates that we should open ourselves up to many opportunities and try many different things. It has been my experience that the spark occurs early in the experience. That doesn't mean that you necessarily reach to fast, but your intuition tells you that you are on to something.

It's a common myth that some people are good at everything or succeed at everything they try. The phenomenon is quite simple, really. They just decide fast if something is or isn't going to work, jettison and quickly forget about the ones that don't. They don't linger and they don't let it bother them. They focus on success and create the illusion that they succeed at everything. Careful analysis will quickly turn up places where they have stubbed their toe. It does happen to them but they just minimize it and move on. Someone who truly succeeds at everything they try, isn't trying enough things.

This is the beauty of selling on Amazon. You can keep your full-time career job for stability and benefits but also provide an additional revenue stream with the goal of ultimately replacing your job for the freedom and flexibility an Amazon business provide. And, you can do it for a relatively small investment compared to conventional businesses.

Hang Tough

Sometimes your positive intuition doesn't meet with immediate success. There's a judgement you make to hang in and continue the fight. Sometimes it takes a while to dial-in but usually there are positive indications pretty early in the process.

It can be difficult to give up on a dream. Occasionally people give up just before a breakthrough… miners that work a stake until they are broke then sell-out for pennies on a dollar only to have the new owners strike it rich almost immediately.

It can be a tough call but all you can do is follow your heart and your hunch. Trust your intuition but do all that you can do minimize the risk. Work with a mentor or coach that has a proven track record of success and allow them to guide you in your journey.

But you must also keep persistence and perseverance in check. We've been taught and trained to stick with things and see them through. I agree with that valuable advice to an extent. But you must be careful not to sink good resources (notably time and money) into a bad cause. A project that's going to fly will usually show some signs of success early on. You must be willing to walk away at some point when something is not working the way it should Sometimes it makes more sense to back up and try a different solution.

Legend has it that the Netflix founder Reed Hastings came up for the idea for the DVD-by-mail rental business because he was late returning a videotape. (When was the last time you inserted a 'real' videotape into a 'real' videotape machine?)

In the mid-Ninteties, he was said to have rented *Apollo 13* from his local Blockbuster Video store and lost it. The penalty for such an infraction was a $40 fine. Here's what Hasting told to a writer for the popular *Fortune Magazine*:

"I remember the fee because I was embarrassed about it. That was back in the VHS days, and it got me thinking that there's a big market out there.

So, I started to investigate the idea of how to create a movie-rental business by mail. I didn't know about DVD's, and then a friend of mine told me they were coming. I ran out to Tower Records in Santa Cruz, California, and mailed CDs to myself, just a disc in an envelope. It was a long 24 hours until the mail arrived back at my house, and I ripped them open and they were all in great shape. That was the big excitement point."

Reed then offered to sell Netflix to Blockbuster—which ultimately didn't happen. Today, everyone watches Netflix and Blockbuster is out of business.

You have to be careful when you set your anchor real deep. And this may include businesses or circumstances where other people are already succeeding. For instance, you may be in a sales position where the top people in the company are doing extremely well but for you, at this particular point in time, in this particular environment, with this particular product and company, it's just not happening despite your best efforts. If you find yourself in a situation like that, my advice is—go try something else.

I can tell you, for me, as I look back over my career, there have been times when I was nothing short of completely stubborn and it cost me dearly. My pride wouldn't let me give up and so I kept pouring myself into something that had huge holes hidden at the bottom. I had total confidence in my own abilities and would not acknowledge outside influences. These can become very costly mistakes, so you have to know when to cut your losses.

If you are old enough to remember film photography, you might be familiar with Kodak. At one time Kodak was the largest film manufacturer in the world. With the introduction of digital cameras to the marketplace, an outside influence (and disruptive one at that) of an entire industry, Kodak refused to accept that digital camera was anything more than a fad.

By the time Kodak realized digital camera were the future—and it was actually film that was becoming obsolete—it was too late. Originally founded in 1888 in Rochester, NY, Kodak filed for Chapter 11 Bankruptcy on January 19, 2012 and moved into the consumer printing business.

The fact of the matter is that in the endeavors where I experienced success, it came pretty quickly. I knew right away. Things felt good. There was a "spark" and I had an immediate sense of "knowing" that success was on the way. Of course, we still had challenges to overcome but the core viability of the idea was proven pretty quickly. Most success (but definitely not all) makes itself known fairly early on in the process. Once you have "proof of concept" you can hunker down for the long haul and employ a "never give up" attitude.

Suspend Fear of Failure

Unless you have many failures, you are unlikely to find success. Sure, there's the occasional "overnight success" (It took me almost 30 years to become an overnight success) but for the most part, successful people try lots of things, or try one thing lots of different ways. It's a trial and error to a large extent. Unfortunately fear of failure holds people back. Even the word "failure" has such a negative connotation. To try is to make a determination. Sometimes when we try we determine that things work well for us. Other times when we try we determine that they don't. Trying something that doesn't work is not to be feared. Never trying to do something that you could be very good at is far worse.

One of the best ways to get over fear is to examine its origin. A source of concern for many people is fear of "looking bad" to relatives, friends and colleagues. We want their approval. We don't want to look foolish. We want to look like we know what we're doing. But this desire for approval should not be allowed to keep us from reaching out to new possibilities. When it comes to personal growth, we all have our comfort zone—that collection of people, places, activities and events where we feel in control. The variables are known. Our skills are documented. Our experience allows us to relax. But growth always requires risk, and naturally we fear risk. We fear loss.

Nothing good comes from your comfort zone.

Your self-esteem cannot be based on "never striking out." Even the greatest baseball players strike out—often. In fact, you can't play the game of baseball without striking out along the way. Typically, the players with the most home runs (and therefore the most swings and attempts), strike out the most. You can't play basketball without missing shots. You can't have a successful business or career without trying some things that don't work. A person with a strong self-image will not be deterred by the fear of failure. Remember, courage is not the absence of fear. It's okay to be a little wary before a new experience. Courage is moving forward in the face of fear. Keep things in perspective and understand that it's not about getting it right the first time, it's just about getting it right.

We learn from things that don't work too, so it's wise to search for the lessons from every experience. Alexander Pope had it right when he said, "We often discover what we will do, by find out what we will not do; which is but saying that he is wiser today than he was yesterday." The only shame in making a mistake is not learning from it.

I've had periods in my life when just about everything I touched turned to gold. I suffered the arrogance of affluence regarding *Outside Influences* but I managed to keep my attribution in check. My thinking regarding *Outside Influences* was fairly well developed and I already had a pretty good appreciation of the influence of factors outside of my control on the circumstances of my life. I did, but those around me did not. When outside influences reversed, and my fortunes fell some, I was fine with it. I understood it was part of the ebb and flow of life and I kept moving forward. My self-image was not based on the home I lived in or my job title and it did not waver.

It was fascinating to watch my friends and colleagues deal with my temporary setbacks. They just weren't sure how to handle them because they didn't understand outside influences. When I talked with them they would be somber and concerned, while I was upbeat and enthusiastic. It warmed my heart because it showed genuine caring on their part and it also helped me to see the need for this book.

One of the keys to keeping fear in check and trying lots of things is to minimize investment of opportunities that cost more than $100,000. Look for an investment in the range of $5,000 to $30,000. That's one of the major benefits of starting an Amazon business. This way fear of failure will not hold you back. Sometimes the greatest risk is not trying, because the possibilities lost might truly have been unlimited while the resources required can be tightly controlled.

I've launched more than one business with a $30,000 investment that ended up being worth many millions.

What is your potential? What are you capable of in your life? These are very important questions and unless you put stress on your capabilities, you will never know their full strength. Outside influences may be poised to lift you to new heights. You'll never know unless you spread your wings and step out of the rest.

Make Hey While the Sun Shines

Outside influences may have you soaring right now, or at some point in the future. If you are in a situation that is working well for you, be extremely careful about making changes. Without question, the best advice I can give you at this circumstance is to pour yourself into it totally and completely. Take advantage of the leverage that's available to you right now. Because of outside influences, it's very possible that the success you are having could be a result of something that is beyond your control (that's not to minimize the importance of your hard work and effort, it just may be a unique moment in time for that particular business), and therefore could be temporary in nature.

There's a rhythm of life created by outside influences. It's why sports teams and companies rise and fall. In many cases, the sports dynasties of a decade ago occupy the cellar in the standings now. There were many former icons of corporate America that have since lost their luster in the marketplace and on Wall Street. And there are many of today that will do so tomorrow. It's inevitable. Think of the euphoria of Toys 'R Us employees felt a couple of years ago as business boomed. Today, Toys 'R Us (in the United States and the UK) is out of business.

A popular business notion today is that of "disruptive technologies." You and your company could very well be the victim of some sort of new technology that renders your product or service useless. Do you remember when you had a land-line in your home or when you would make a call from a phone-booth?

For the fifty years taxi cabs dominated the streets of New York city a sea of yellow could be seen everywhere, around the clock, with a monopoly on an industry. Enter Uber. Enter Lyft. Both of these companies—now in the conscious mind of an entire industry—has changed everything.

In addition to new technologies, many other outside influences could shift unbeknownst to you, and disrupt your success. Oftentimes, these "shifts" happen when things look the brightest and you seem the least vulnerable.

So, drive hard when you're in a situation where the dollars are flowing well... keep it going and pour yourself into it. Release the brakes and make hay while the sun shines. Work the crazy hours and fortify your next egg. Thinking of your circumstance as temporary will propel you to do a lot of the right things. It will inject urgency. And, it will encourage you to be careful with your money. Be sure to set a significant portion aside and invest it cautiously. I know it may seem that the good times will never end, and hopefully they won't, but if they do you will be very glad that you were conservative with your dollars and protected yourself and your family. Recognize that, to an extent, factors beyond you have created this wonderful situation and realize that a twist of forces could negate it in an instant. Watch out for the arrogance of affluence. Don't become its victim, for it can burn you if you're not careful.

Success Breeds Success

Outside influences can converge with your own talent, ability and hard work to create leverage. Leverage is usually necessary for big time success. It multiplies the effect of your efforts. Leverage expands your capability and increases your potential. It's the thing that can keep you on top once you climb up there. Leverage is a vital tool of successful people. Once you've been successful, you can oftentimes leverage that success and dramatically reduce (but not eliminate) the risks of other ventures.

Success creates resources. The signs of success become a self-fulfilling prophecy. Resources can create more momentum. Momentum can provide the force needed to push new concepts and bring new ideas to fruition. Once you've established momentum, the speed of success reduces potential challenges to little more than bumps in the road. In marketing, it's understood that, the more you sell, the more you sell. The momentum keeps building and negative outside influences are kept in check while positive ones are engaged and leveraged. When it all comes together it's a wonderful thing, indeed.

A Noble Character

Good people bring dignity and professionalism to their work, not the other way around. Quality of effort is its own reward. It's pragmatic to understand that others must see our contribution in order to justify our compensation, but beyond that, work is about self-satisfaction. It's what we bring to it that matters, not whatever inherently resides there. We've all come into contact with high quality people in low paying positions that distinguish themselves via reliability, integrity and attention to detail. Likewise, we've had to contact with so-called professionals that leave us confused and dissatisfied. It's what you do from a position of prestige that determines your own personal level of appreciation from others.

We can all learn from the tradition of the craftsman, a person dedicated to producing fine workmanship. A person who is motivated first and foremost by doing good work even if no one else will ever see it. That's an approach that has tapped into the rhythm of life.

Our character manifests itself every day in our work and in how we treat and relate to others. Our character is the vessel of our motivations. From it springs forth who we are and what we're all about and what we wish to accomplish in any situation. Integrity comes from being true to oneself. It's when our character, our motives and our behavior are all in alignment and are open and straightforward for all to see.

Courageous people are drawn to a noble cause. The purity of the flight magnifies the appeal. Dedication to excellence is the hallmark of a person of high ideals that becomes self-evident in everything you do.

Catalytic Concepts

- Outside influences are creating opportunities everywhere, every day.
- We have not been given a limited number of chances for success in life. We can, and should, try lots of things. The more things we try and test, the greater the odds that a working combination of factors will come together.

- We've got to be judicious in our application of persistence to this aspect of life or we may stay with an inappropriate situation at the expense of one with significant potential.
- We must break through fear of failure. We shouldn't fear attempting new things, as simply to have tried shows our inner strength. Furthermore, every experience yields value, if we are open to the lessons.
- The more things we try, the greater our possibility of success.
- When a successful situation presents itself, we should stay focused and maximize our return.
- Our character manifests in our work and the craftsman presents a wonderful role model.

CHAPTER 14

Future Influences

"I believe that in the end the truth will conquer."
–John Wycliffe

The Value of Knowledge

It's inherent in all of us to desire success and to seek the truth—the ultimate knowledge of who we are and what life is all about. The interplay of these two desires is fascinating. Understanding *Outside Influences* sheds light on the underlying dynamics of the knotty system in which we live, work, and play. We want the best that life has to offer and most of us are prepared to work for it. We follow the well-known rules and pay the generally accepted price of admission. We want to get into the inner circle of life's elite. We are fascinated by the abundance and freedom they enjoy. We want all of the best for our families and ourselves.

Developing your understanding of outside influences is an ongoing process but the benefits to be gained from doing so are substantial. Surely, life will always present challenges and mysteries, but many riddles will be solved for you once you see the far-reaching effects of factors beyond your control. If you've been open as you read this book, I think you're going to find that you will revisit the ideas of *Outside Influences* even if you've rejected them, because the evidence will keep confronting you. It's everywhere. If it all makes sense to you, it will settle in and become part of the framework through which you view the world.

The previously existing and widely accepted approaches to dealing with the effects of outside influences have been to minimize and ignore them, or to build a belief structure that supersedes them. Responsible consideration renders these approaches inappropriate at best. Denial is a response to fear. We fear outside influences because we are confronted with the tragic and dramatic examples of their intrusion on our lives. The sheer power and magnitude of certain catastrophic events pierces our armor, but the day-to-day evidence doesn't get through. Furthermore, the positive effects of random events and other influences get attributed to our talent, ability, and overall value as a special human being. As a result, the only ones we acknowledge are the ones that cause us pain, so we try to build additional barriers.

Mature, enlightened people are curious about the world and want to understand its dynamic forces. They are comfortable that they will be able to deal with what they find and they are correct in that assertion. To function based on misinformation is dangerous. Knowledge, even if it doesn't appear readily actionable, is always the antidote for the position of ignorance.

We want the truth and we deserve the truth. Consider the biggest discovery (truth) mankind has ever made about our planet. You know, a lot of really smart people thought the world was flat for a very long time. It could be argued that knowing, as we do now, that the earth is round, makes virtually zero difference to the vast majority of us in our day-to-day lives. Yet, few of us would want to labor under the misconception of a flat earth. We know intuitively that bad information leads to bad decisions.

Knowing the shape of the world is one thing, but knowing the influence of outside factors on our world is quite another. Outside influences come into play with a high degree of regularity in our lives. Someone who knows and understands this is better able to cope, even if the knowledge does not necessarily suggest any immediate shifts in how we approach the world. For sure, once you understand and accept the concept of outside influences, you will never see the world in quite the same way again.

Understanding outside influences puts many of the events on our world into perspective. We're freed of the notion that everything happens for a reason. That idea can provide a warm and fuzzy feeling sometimes, but it can also become a huge burden. Even the most creative among us can be challenged to fabricate a reason for certain events. Understanding that randomness is an underlying dynamic force in nature, and in our lives, answers many questions. Realizing that some factors are beyond our control puts greater emphasis on properly handling the ones that are within our reach.

The ideas in *Outside Influences* are understood best if they are discussed, debated and argued. You will find that you understand them better a year from now than immediately after finishing the book. As Michel de Montaigne said, "It is good to rub and polish our brain against that of others." Even if you never discuss it with anyone, you will see the evidence in your day-to-day life. You'll have that "Ah ha' experience when an event demonstrates the incredible randomness of life. Like seeds, the ideas will slowly germinate and grow. Give them time. Try to get into the habit of observing the outside influences that affect your life (How did you hear about this book?). They are all around you and happen many times each day. Most have little or no effect, but some can be life changing.

The Serendipity of Success

Knowledge is its own reward but there are other advantages to understanding the effect of *Outside Influences*. Clearly, understanding how the world works better prepares you to function in it. Denying or superseding the reality with our complex belief systems surely does not give us any advantage.

Yet, to a degree life is an adventure that happens to us as opposed to being unilaterally directed, created and forged by us. Understanding this engenders a sense of wonder and anticipation as each day offers opportunities for exploration and expansion. It is a lovely thing to watch life unfold and to set our sails and rudder as dictated by the winds and currents.

People who have little faith in the noble nature of mankind have been afraid to acknowledge outside influences for fear that people would abdicate responsibility for their lives. That is neither the recommended nor the likely response to this awareness. *Outside Influences* starts with a high concept of people and belief in their passion and motivation. People who get it know that they must still take personal responsibly and they open themselves up to the possibilities of the universe. In many ways these ideas increase motivation, or at least the ability to maintain motivation, because they accept that things don't always turn out as intended. Since that's understood, when problems occur, which they often do, people are better able to cope and keep trying. They don't feel like a failure, only that the particular thing they tried didn't work out.

Almost everything beneficial we've been taught and have believed about achieving success has been designed to do one thing, get us to try and keep trying. Just as many of us were told as children, if you're good little girls and boys, Santa Claus is going to bring you some nice toys on Christmas. Our parents told us that with good intentions even though it was not exactly true. So, too, we were told the stories about the keys to success. They are told to us with our own best interests at heart and they do occasionally lead to success, to keep up trying in the face of adversity. It's simple really; success is most of the result of thousands of small experiments. It's trial and error to the nth degree until the right formula is uncovered. It can be hard to determine the effects of outside influences, but you can always rest assured they are there.

Better yet, if you can find someone that has the formula for success—and you can replicate it—you can speed up the steps necessary to find your own success. And while following a proven formula doesn't guarantee success, that formula might just be the outside influence you need.

Remember, the one thing all successful experiences have in common is that somebody tried something. Beyond that, you may be able to identify certain common traits in successful people, but nothing is universal except trying. Successful people come from all backgrounds and all walks of life. They see the world quite differently and they understand the path to success in different ways. That's the beauty of it—success is available to everybody, as long as you keep trying. It's a combination lock and the best thing to do is keep turning the dial. And when you can find someone who can "give you" the combination, success will be open to yu—then you can explain to everybody the keys to your success.

Healthy Skepticism

Until you find that mentor, coach or the person that can give you the "secret code", I recommend a healthy skepticism regarding the opinions and ideas of others. I'm not saying you should reject their advice without consideration, but I am saying that you should keep in mind that it may be flawed. Without intention, they may leave out a critical piece of the puzzle. However similar, rest assured there are differences between them and you and between their situation and yours. Or they many have ulterior motives for wanting to modify your behavior. Always find and work with someone that has a proven track record for success and has your best interest at heart.

Gut instincts are often right on target. The psychology is in your favor when you believe in what you are doing—when your actions are consistent with your thinking and values.

Understanding the human tendency toward attribution prepares you to be a well-informed listener. Take things with a grain of salt. The validity of any piece of advice cannot be known for you, in your situation, at this time in your life, until you put it into place and try it out. Obviously, you can't try everything, so you've got to be judicious. Remember it's okay to disagree, even with someone who has achieved high levels of success. By the same token, stay open to concepts from all directions, above, sideways, and below. Considering the source may be somewhat helpful in evaluating advice, but be careful not to discount an idea that could prove very beneficial. You never know where good counsel may come from, so you've got to keep your antenna up.

Oftentimes people give their particular "secrets" in a passing phrase. It's usually not that they are trying to hide anything; it's just that they many actually realize the significance of a particular point. The person intent on success learns to listen carefully and probe appropriately. Asking for additional information on a certain facet of an idea can yield some great information.

The ideas of others serve us best as catalysts in our own thinking rather than to be taken whole, as it. Ultimately, you synthesize all the concepts and experiences that come to you, coupling them with your ideation. You forge these ideas into your own workable plan and philosophical approach. That' what you'll take to your work each day and that's what you'll juxtapose against the prevailing outside influences of that time and place. You'll take your best shot, keep your fingers crossed and have a backup plan ready.

Trials and Tribulations

In the grand scheme of things almost all setbacks are temporary. And, a setback is a setup for a comeback. "This too will pass" is sound advice and it pays to keep things in perspective. Problems and difficulties often have hidden opportunities within them. Almost always they present the chance to achieve personal growth by facing and dealing with them. We make our bodies stronger by lifting heavy weights. So it is with our character.

It's quite common for surviving cancer patients to look back on their ordeal and refer to it as a learning experience, often in warm terms. Having faced so much suffering, pain and fear, they realize they emerged stronger and wiser. They have an enhanced sense of meaning and importance of life and their value system often shifts back to what most people acknowledge as the truly important things. A person never so tested does not have the benefit of the experience. Almost all such trials carry the benefit of strengthening your inner self. Success is so much sweeter when you have to really work for it.

I know that at times life can beat on you and cause pain and anguish. Don't fall prey to the debilitating drain of self-pity. Life has its twists and turns and outside influences have no agenda or ulterior motives. They just are and life just is and things happen to most everyone from time to time. If you've hit upon some bad luck, keep your composure, don't waste energy bemoaning your fate. Focus on your objectives and keep working. The ground will shift again and outside influences may provide the wind you need to soar (or at least stop blowing at gale force in your face.)

Why, the Audacity!

Here's a secret: outside influences are very democratic. Like "Justice" they are blind. They evolve and flow and opportunities blossom and fade. Remember, the one thing all super-successes have in common is that they tried something. More often than not, they tried something BIG. It usually takes about the same amount of energy to go for the big time as it does to go for a conservative, reasonable goal. Many people never give themselves a chance at big time success. In all of the lotteries across the world, no one has ever won who did not buy a ticket. And no one has ever hit big time success without giving something big a try. The fact is, most people never even get into the big-time game. They eliminate themselves before anything even gets started and that dramatically increases the odds for those who do try.

The world is full of unlikely success stories, like the businessperson who drops out of college without a degree but still builds a big business (and could even become the richest person in the world). The athlete who contracts cancer but still performs at the highest levels of competition (and perhaps wins the Tour de France). The homely person with the beautiful spouse is another example. Life is full of examples of what can happen if you try, and none of these or countless other successes would ever have happened if these people hadn't tried.

The limiting effects of our surroundings and experience can be difficult to overcome. Most people, so beat up by society and exhausted from working the old paradigm of success, have lost their enthusiasm for trying. Their belief in the law of compensation and unwillingness to acknowledge outside influences has left them frustrated and confused. They get used up and discarded by corporations after a lifetime of service. The fact of the matter is, to some degree, it was unfair of them to believe that hard work alone would yield all that life has to offer, or at least it was uninformed.

Open up to possibilities and go for the big time! Take a shot at something extraordinary! Of course, there is no guarantee of success, but so what? Limit your exposure, but get into the game! Try something! Start an Amazon business—get a coach and mentor and incorporate a proven system and software tools. You never know what might happen. One thing is certain, if you don't try, nothing big will happen. It's exciting follow a system and achieve success. Follow your dreams and don't let the disapproval of others dissuade you.

The publishing of *Outside Influences* is an example. I look at it this way; this book is my baby. It's the results of decades of thinking an analysis. I genuinely believe that it has a better chance for massive success if I'm involved. Most writers are writers. They want to pass the book off to someone else and let that person (or company) handle all the "mess" of sales and customers and stuff like that. Some authors today use a book as a "funnel", give it away free, simply for the purpose of upselling you thousands of dollars of add-on information. Not me. As I said before, I love people and I want to engage with as many people as possible.

I have a unique platform. I'm fortunate to have the opportunity to share this message with thousands of people (and more) every month, live and in person. I'm passionate about this topic and perhaps I will end up being an outside influence for the people who read it.

Will outside influences affect the sale of the book and the ultimate success it achieves? Of course! Maybe someone who knows Oprah or Ellen will read and enjoy *Outside Influences*. Perhaps the current prevailing attitude in politics are "ready" for this message as we have a president who tweets messages in an uncommon (and some would say "unpresidential) way. It could be that videos, quotes, and endorsements get posted on Instagram, Facebook, YouTube and other relevant social media platforms. I'm going to do everything I can to promote the book and get the word out but I realize that for big time success, for millions of copies to be sold, to achieve best seller status, things outside of my control and comprehension will have to work in my favor. In the meantime, I'll be having a heck of a lot of fun. It's exhilarating to bring a project to fruition and receive such positive feedback from the people who are exposed to it.

When Your Ship Comes In

When you do realize significant success, keep the likely effects of outside influences in mind. Sure, you will have labored mightily and you'll deserve some accolades and attention, but don't overdo it and don't let the people around you overdo it.

In a sense, reading *Outside Influences* has robbed you. You can't fall prey to the arrogance of affluence or the pompous triviality that seems so well deserved when you vanquish your foes and emerge victorious. A parade might be fitting, huh? Perhaps a statue? In fact, if you've hit the "big time", significant personal success, perhaps wealth, you haven't hit a hole in one; you've hit several, in just one round of golf. Incredible! You are good, dude (or dudette), real good. Now, let me see you do it again.

Success can be intoxicating. You may be down to earth and pragmatic now but focus in on the things that matter most to provide a tether. Remember, it is not about getting and keeping things. Speed kills and so does flying too high— just ask Icarus.

I have an idea. Why not stay with your feet planted on terra firma in the first place?

It's a foregone conclusion that your pending (or past) success will depend on: talent, hard work, insight, risk taking, dedication, professionalism, persistence, leadership, motivation, attitude, creativity, and brilliance... all very true. But there will also be outside influences and random events.

In just about every culture on the planet, in just about every spoken language, when we're saying goodbye to someone and they're going to be off on an endeavor of some sort, what do we say in addition to goodbye? We say, "Good luck." We say that for a reason.

When you hit it big, if you do, be humble and be thankful. Be a big enough person to accept the limitations of your own internal influence as well as the influences of things, which may even be outside of your awareness or comprehension. In doing so, you'll demonstrate a knowledge and wisdom that will really set you apart.

In the Absence of Big Time Success

And if your ship remains lost at sea, as many do, remember the enjoyment of the ride. Remember to honor the effort and value yourself and your contributions to the world. Remember that part of what it takes for big time success is beyond your control; so don't torture yourself for not being able to produce something that is out of your control in the first place.

I know that sometimes the waiting game is brutal. Life is short and it's good to be impatient for success. I've observed that the Doppler Effect works on how we perceive time. You remember the Doppler Effect? It's the thing that makes the sound of an oncoming train seem different when it's approaching than after it's passed. The train is emitting the exact same sound all the way along its route, but it sounds quite different to us (it has to do with the speed of sound waves and the effects of the train's speed on them). Life works this way on our perception of time. As we anticipate future events we're excited about, an upcoming vacation perhaps, the days and weeks seem to drag on, almost like time is moving in slow motion. Yet, when we look back in time, events of many years ago seem like only yesterday. The time compresses in retrospect. Likewise, waiting for your ship to come in may seem like an eternity. That's why it makes sense to look for the good in what you do each day. Find enjoyment and fulfillment in your work. But be on the lookout for outside influences to come together and create opportunities. And be ready to take advantage of them when they do.

What's Average?

Human beings are extraordinary organisms. One of the key notions of this book is that we all possess all of the qualities necessary for big time success. Of course, we will not all achieve it but that will seldom be due to the fact that a person is fundamentally lacking in some meaningful way. I think people—all people—are fascinating and full of potential. A fundamental premise of this book is that success is open to all of us. An "average" person can achieve above average success, it doesn't only go to the beautiful people, or the brilliant people. It can and does happen to regular people all of the time, if you are open to it.

Stick with the Basics

Your contribution to your own success need not emerge from some fancy complicated formula. Stick with the basics. To distinguish yourself above the crowd be reliable and professional. Do good work and be a good person. Be honest. Have fun. Seek knowledge and personal growth. Have confidence tempered with humility. Keep balance in your life. Care about people. Cherish children and respect the elderly. Be focused and value time. Hone your interpersonal communications skills (speaking, writing and listening). Stay true to yourself. Bind all of that together with a true dedication to excellence that is readily identifiable in all that you do, and you're well on your way.

Don't get caught up in the latest motivational craze. There's nothing mysterious about it. The common-sense fundamentals are what you need. You probably practice this approach already. The key is to honor the effort you put forth each day, try lots of things, and position yourself so that outside influences can get under your wings and provide lift.

The Wonder of it All

It all boils down to your life intersecting with opportunity and then making the most of it. Just like an experienced fisherman knows there are fish in the sea and will eventually find them, you know, with certainty, that outside influences are constantly realigning and opportunities are constantly emerging. It's a rich bubbling broth full of exciting places to focus your energy, talent and ability.

There are opportunities everywhere but you've got to learn to look for them and make an effort to do so. Being of an entrepreneurial bias, I will advise you to consider some sort of business of your own, but it need not be an expensive proposition and it need not be full-time. It could be a small, part-time endeavor that only takes a few hours a week but still has the potential to hit big for you. A business of your own adds equity to the equation and that makes it far more potent than any job can be. You can sit and wish for things to happen or you can take a shot. My approach is straightforward: if I'm not actively working on something that has huge potential, I'm actively looking for something to work on that has huge potential. Life is too short to just hang out—and there's too much opportunity out there—I want some of it! Don't you?

You will draw opportunity to you if you build a reputation as an accomplished professional. I get several calls every month from people with new business ideas they want to run by me (supposedly to get my opinions, but they hope to get my attention and interest). When people know you can produce, they seek you out. And you should always find time to listen because some of the ideas they run by you will be million dollar ideas.

Being aware of outside influences is a very good thing. It expands our understanding of how the world works. This knowledge provides a framework to function better and achieve more. Beyond that, it's comforting to know that despite the effects of things outside of our control, our own drive and initiative provide the power that moves us forward.

In the measurement of our own performance, one thing can be said: There's always room for improvement. That's been one of the most empowering ideas for me throughout my career. Even now, after 30+ years in the business world, I can still improve. I can still get better at what I do. Personal growth has been a constant for me. I've walked away from some pretty lucrative things because I felt stagnant. It's a wonderful gift of life that we never have to stop learning.

You build a successful life and career from the inside out. If you want more success, make yourself worthy of more success. Make yourself more valuable by acquiring more knowledge or improving and expanding your skills. Opportunities expand to fill our capabilities. Capable people can transform circumstances and leverage benefit from even meager opportunities.

There are no limits! Within "the system" the power to achieve is virtually unlimited. Major forces are coming together all of the time and waves of opportunity they create are massive in their proportions. For all its limitations, the world is a wonderful place and it's teeming with opportunity for all of us if we just watch for outside influences and then, ride the wave.

Fare Thee Well

Life is fascinating and also challenging. How we think about and understand events matters greatly in our ability to thrive. The ideas expressed here have helped me in negotiating life's twists and turns. I want them to help you in some way as well.

Part of the real fun in life is discovery. How fortunate we are to live in a world that facilitates the free-flow of ideas. Learning is a life-long process and it's fascinating to reach out to new conceptual horizons. I hope reading *Outside Influences* has been such an experience for you.

In closing let me thank you for taking time to digest these ideas. I invite you to share with me in observing the elegant beauty of the randomness in life as it unfolds and presents its unlimited possibilities each day. Be sure to find me on Social Media and share your "Ah Ha's" as you experience the power of outside influences.

Good luck, my friend!

About the Author

Adam Ginsberg is the #1 Amazon sales trainer in the world and an internationally renowned speaker on leadership, success, entrepreneurship social media, and e-commerce. Adam's straight-shooting viewpoints on the business have made him a valuable resource for media seeking commentary and insights on real topics that matter. He has appeared on *Fox Business, CNBC, World News Tonight, The Today Show*, and *MSNBC*.

Printed in the USA
CPSIA information can be obtained
at www.ICGtesting.com
JSHW082341140824
68134JS00020B/1814

9 781642 794779